On GOOD BEHAVIOR

Questions and Answers for
Solving and Preventing
Dog Problems

BARDI McLENNAN

HOWELL BOOK HOUSE

New York

Macmillan General Reference
A Prentice Hall Macmillan Company
15 Columbus Circle
New York, NY 10023

Howell Book House

MACMILLAN is a registered trademark of Macmillan, Inc.

Library of Congress Cataloging-in-Publication Data

McLennan, Bardi.
        On good behavior: questions and answers for solving and
preventing dog problems / Bardi McLennan.
                p.   cm.
        Includes bibliographical references and index.
        ISBN 0-87605-667-2
        1. Dogs--Behavior--Miscellanea.   I. Title.
SF433.M35   1995
636.7'088'7--dc20   94-48611
                                                                      CIP

Manufactured in the United States of America
10 9 8 7 6 5 4 3 2 1

CONTENTS

ACKNOWLEDGMENTS

The field of dog behavior is without absolutes. No one be-havior modification works in an identical fashion on every dog, with every owner, so feedback from those owners is an essential part of future success. To that end, I extend my sin-cere thanks to all the people who have been good enough to keep me informed of their progress.

My thanks also to my editor, Marcy Zingler, who stirs up the "terrier" in me to tackle bigger obstacles than I think I can handle.

To Sian Cox for coming through once again with a perfect book cover and to Jan Walker for her artistic sense of canine behavior and humor in all the wonderful illustrations through-out the book.

—Bardi McLennan
Weston, Connecticut

Once you let a dog into your life, you want the world to know it.

INTRODUCTION

There are two ways a dog owner can use this book. First, if you know what your dog's behavior problem is, you can go directly to that chapter for guidance. All are commonly asked questions, so chances are you'll find the answers there. Keep in mind that behaviors (good and bad) tend to overlap. In dealing with any animal's behavior, it's the "one thing leads to another" theory—in full-blown action! So the second way to find the answers to your questions is to browse.

Beware of falling into that most common trap of "trying everything," which is invariably followed by the complaint that "nothing worked." Give one remedy an honest chance before moving on to another suggestion. Don't expect a one-week miracle to erase an unacceptable behavior that the dog has perfected over a period of years. It often takes many *months* to see substantial improvement.

Rufus does not consider a behavior to be unacceptable if that is how he has managed to coexist within the family circle until now. Perhaps Rufus has even succeeded in running the group. Changing from one method to another will confuse the dog, and no doubt you'll be faced with one of the more frustrating canine behaviors, known as "selective hearing." The dog will pick up on your flip-flopping, turn a deaf ear to your latest demand and wait to see what your next offer may be. Your goal should be reeducation, not entertainment!

In the meantime, Rufus will continue to misbehave. If you think you've been working on the problem without making any impression, you may just have been making the wrong impression. Dogs will settle for any form of attention they can get, including shouting, cursing or physical punishment. As long as they get some reaction, they'll continue whatever behavior elicits it. Not because dogs like the abuse, but because they have a basic need for social interaction, and secondly because the outcome is predictable. *Dogs thrive on consistency.*

TWO SIDES TO EVERY QUESTION

When a dog's behavior is a problem, there are plenty of Questions, and to most of these there are Answers. But take heart— *before* problems arise, *before* there's a need for Answers, there are Preventions. You will find that in this book both are given in reply to each Question, so if your dog hasn't yet succumbed to some terrible misconduct, you will benefit from the Prevention part of the discussion. As I mentioned, unacceptable behaviors build up, overlap or develop from one form into another, so don't skip the Prevention tips just because they don't happen to apply *today*. Tomorrow could be here before you know it!

Many Answers and Preventions refer to Obedience training, not because I think such instruction is a panacea for all that ails every dog/owner relationship, but because it is the easiest starting point for you both. Behavioral problems often arise from a misunderstanding of what makes a dog tick, or what stupid, unthinking little things we humans do to *cause* the very problems we complain about. Obedience training in a class with a "good" instructor (I'll explain what I mean by that in a moment) is a first step in learning how to read your dog correctly and in forming a relationship that relies heavily on two-way trust.

I prefer classes to private instruction for basic training because you and your dog will benefit from being with other people and dogs, hearing other people's problems and giving the dog much-needed socialization. Of course, some people lead such social lives themselves that this aspect of the class is not a necessary consideration. However, many who lead a more solitary existence are also the people who acquire dogs to break the loneliness and provide companionship. They are the ones who desperately need Obedience classes.

Let's get back to what I mean by a good instructor. I mean one who teaches lots more than the basic commands of Heel, Sit, Down, Stay and Come; a teacher who knows that instilling confidence in both the dog and the owner is the basis for establishing trust, and that trust comes only when the training is 100 percent consistent, firm and fair. A good instructor tells you, then shows you, then teaches you how to teach your dog.

A good teacher acknowledges that for every dog in the class, there is a human being also attached to the lead who will probably know less than the dog at the end of each session and who needs help in understanding *why* these things are being taught. A good teacher explains that each command word is only a tool that enables you to begin to communicate with your dog and to establish a level of trust with your dog. A good teacher then takes you to that level of communication and understanding.

A good teacher is never rough, tough or loud and does not allow that kind of behavior from anyone in the class.

Let me give you an example of an Obedience command used as a tool. Teaching a dog to Sit on command is not a lesson in how to feed your dog cookies or one to teach you how to say "Good Dog." It is a tool. You can use it as a Prevention by telling your dog "Sit" *before* it jumps up on people, *before* you open the front door, *as* you stop to chat with friends on the street, etc. The same thing applies to all the other things you and Rufus or Roxanne learn in Obedience class. They are one-word commands that are easy for you to remember and for the dog to put together with the appropriate response. Once Rufus makes the right connection between a word and an action, he will be basking in the warm, loving sound of "Good Dog" instead of getting (or worse, seeking) negative attention.

All dogs need to hear far fewer "Nos" and many more "Good Dogs."

1

PUPPIES

Let's begin with puppies, since that's where most dog owners begin. Unfortunately, this is where problems can also begin, because pups are so ready and eager to learn absolutely everything, and learn they do—whether purposely instructed by the owner or self-taught. A puppy spends every waking minute absorbing every conceivable thing about each person in the family—every gesture, every footstep, changes in every person's tone of voice, everyone's routine, all the smells and sounds. In the process, the pup finds his own niche in the family.

The owner of an older dog will also benefit from starting here, because not too long ago those adult dogs were pups and just maybe that's how far back you'll have to go to discover where things went wrong to cause a problem you have today. Knowing how it all began won't solve what is currently wrong, but you'll see how the process works and have a better understanding of how innocently unwanted behavior can start. You'll definitely learn how to avoid making the same mistakes with your next puppy!

"Begin at the beginning."
"Oh, all right. 'Once upon a time'..."

Puppy Basics 101 consists of crate training, housetraining and confinement. While each is individually important, the three go hand in hand to form one solid base on which you will build all future training in order to have a well-behaved pet. Whenever we teach, we learn. As the pup learns the rules and routines of a new home, the owner also learns a lot about the pup. However, it's only fair to warn you that puppies are quicker at this game than people, and soon learn to exploit the concept!

CRATE TRAINING

Make life easier for yourself and your puppy. *Get the crate before you get the dog.* There are several valid reasons to do so:

- You need to learn how to open and close the door. (Don't laugh—not all crates are the same, nor are all easy to operate.)
- You need to decide where the crate will be kept during the day and in which bedroom at night.
- You also need to figure out where, or if, the crate will fit in the car.

Two types are available. One is made of wire so the dog can see out, you can see in and air can circulate freely. The other is made of sturdy molded plastic and is commonly referred to as an "airline" crate. An old folded bath towel makes perfect bedding in either one. When the pup has outgrown accidents and chewing, you can get a fancy mattress and fancy dog beds elsewhere in the house, but not now. Keep the crate out of direct sunlight, away from drafts and sources of heat or air conditioning. Cover the wire crate (except for the door) to make it snug and more denlike at night.

Introduce your pup to the crate gently and cheerfully. One way is to encourage her to run in after a toy or small treat.

When the puppy has gone in and out several times, say "Crate" in a happy voice as the pup enters the crate, then close the door, but leave it closed only for a minute or two the first few times. Make no comment when the pup comes out. Ignore her fussing and only let the puppy out when she is quiet.

Set up a schedule that fits your own, but be sure the puppy has eliminated before expecting her to stay in the crate for any length of time. A young puppy (two to six months) should not be left in the crate for more than a couple of hours, except overnight. When the dog is older, housebroken and accustomed to being crated, about four hours should be the daytime limit.

Entice your pup to walk into the crate . . .

. . . and he'll soon go in without "assistance."

HOUSETRAINING

Take the pup outside *on leash* last thing at night. As the pup eliminates, say "Good dog," and then it's into the crate for the night with a small good-night, good-dog biscuit. In the morning, barking or squeaking are signals for you to leap into action! Take the shortest route from the crate to get the puppy outside, always on leash so you are there to say "Good dog." This is *not* a walk. It is *not* playtime. It is *not* time for chitchat. This is just part of Puppy Basics 101.

The day's routine is approximately: Eliminate, Play, Eat, Eliminate, Sleep, Eliminate, Play, Eat, Eliminate, Sleep, etc. The exact schedule depends primarily upon your own, but also on the age of the dog, the type of food, how many meals you feed per day and thus how many times your puppy must eliminate.

CONFINEMENT

Dog owners have at last been won over to crate training, but are still amazed at the long list of benefits that come with it. Housetraining has been essential since the day a caveman first said, "Okay dog, come on in." But now we come to the concept of confinement, and it's surprising how many dog owners think that, once housetrained, Rufus should have what is mistakenly referred to as "freedom of the house" when left alone for anything from ten minutes to all day. It is invariably an unkind form of liberty, which more accurately means "freedom to get into trouble."

If there's no responsible person available to keep a sharp eye out for an hour or so, put the pup in the crate with a toy. But when it's a question of leaving a puppy alone for a long shopping spree, or a normal workday, then different plans must be made for confinement so the puppy is safe—and your other possessions are, too!

The kitchen is generally the best area for confinement. The floor is washable and it's a relatively easy room to puppy-proof.

1. Remove scatter rugs or mats.
2. Put electrical cords out of reach.
3. Remove the garbage, the trash and anything of personal value.
4. Put childproof locks on cabinets that a curious paw or nose could easily pry open.
5. Use a pet gate in the doorway.
6. Leave a radio on low volume, maybe in another room.
7. Secure the dog's crate door *open* by means of a strong metal snap. (Do not use string or rope, which will be chewed.)
8. Fill the water bowl.
9. Leave a small treat or two along with some toys.
10. Change the toy assortment every few days so there's variety, but hold back on quantity!

When you aren't there, confinement *is the* Prevention *for punishment.*

Now you've got it! *Confinement!*

The dog will be perfectly content with this arrangement, and when you come home you'll put the key in the door knowing you'll be greeted by a good little puppy that did not destroy most of your favorite things.

There is actually even more to confinement than this, in connection with separation anxiety. But we're getting ahead of ourselves.

Question: "My Springer puppy is four months old and is fine except for two things. He chews my belongings and also my hands. I've tried saying no firmly, but it doesn't work. What can I do?"

Answer: Just saying no isn't enough when dealing with a pup. As soon as you've said "No," you have to teach whatever will produce a behavior that earns a "Good Dog."

Prevention: Keep a puppy and your belongings apart—far apart! Pups can only chew what they can get in their mouths. As for hands, see Chapter 7 for how to teach pups to inhibit their own bites.

Question: "We have a Toy Fox Terrier and she won't stop licking our hands. It was cute at first, but has become a real nuisance!"

Answer: There are two things you can do. Stop the licking (now that it's a bad habit) by putting a little Grannick's Bitter Apple on the back of your hands. Allow the dog to lick as usual, but as she does, say "No lick!", stand up, fold your arms and turn away. Ignore. I know—that's three corrections, but licking is hard to cure.

Prevention: Puppies lick hands (and faces when available) because that is how they naturally beg for food and attention from their mother. It's a submissive attention-getter (look at poor little ol' me—starved for food and love), and because it is cute and appeals to our own nurturing instincts, it's hard to turn down. Stop when it's still cute, before it becomes a nuisance. (Licking requires medical intervention when it results in self-mutilation.)

Question: "I'd like to take my year-old Miniature Schnauzer with me wherever I go, but she urinates when anyone (even friends) speak to her or try to pet her. I've tried having her greet people outdoors, but it doesn't help. The only time she controls herself is if I pick her up. Will she outgrow this?"

Answer: This is a problem with a name. It's called submissive urination and it is quite common in female puppies and more prevalent in certain breeds (Cocker Spaniels, for one). Some puppies outgrow it, but a year is beyond the limit. Don't wait any longer.

Do not pick her up and pay no attention to puddles. If you are angry or upset by the dog's act of submission, you will force her to try to be more submissive. You and your friends can help. For now, ask everyone to ignore the dog. Put her on a Sit-Stay when you meet friends on the street. Ask people to smile at her, but *not* to reach out to touch the dog. When the dog initiates greeting people in your home, the response should be low key.

Prevention: Certain submissive behaviors in dogs, such as deference to a larger, older or dominant dog, are basic to self-preservation. Two circumstances bring on submissive urination, however: a person standing or bending over the dog, and hands reaching down to pet the dog. Preventing those actions that cause the dog to be submissive will help to overcome it.

Question: "I adopted a ten-month-old Sheltie, and whenever we meet another dog, she rolls over on her back and urinates. She's not a nervous dog. Will Obedience school help with this?"

Answer: See the previous Answer. An Obedience instructor can help get the dog over this by using a Saturation process and the cooperation of all the dogs in the class (see Chapter 8).

Prevention: Same as previous Prevention.

Question: "I adopted an older puppy and can't get her to tell me when she needs to go outside. I've stuck her nose in her mess in the house. I've slapped her rear end and told her she's a bad dog. Every time we go outside, I use the words 'Potty outside,' but she doesn't get it. Should I take her back to the shelter?"

Answer: *No!* Hang in there, but change your tactics. Forget about sticking the dog's nose in it and forget about spanking. *Teach, don't punish.* Once the accident has happened, give the dog a Time-out while you take care of cleaning it up—in silence and with a deodorizing cleanser made for the purpose.

Prevention: With any adopted dog, it is sometimes necessary to go back to a young puppy schedule. Take her out every half hour. Say "Outside" as you reach for the leash and again as you open the door. No chatter. Go to the same spot and stand there. Praise as she eliminates. If after ten minutes the dog has not relieved herself, go back inside (no chatter, no scolding), put her in the crate, wait five minutes and take her out again.

Question: "I have a three-month-old Silky Terrier that eats its own stools. I've had dogs for twenty-five years and have never run into this problem before, although my veterinarian says all dogs do it and there's no way to stop it. Should I get rid of this little dog while he's still a puppy and I might recoup my money?"

Answer: Don't give up! It's not the end of the world! The cure is as easy as walking your puppy *on leash,* which is the best way to housetrain anyway. Don't give him the opportunity to eat stool. As he turns toward it, say "Yuck!" or "Leave it!" and lead the dog away. Clean up *immediately.* Break the habit in this way for a few months and be quick to poop-scoop for a few more months. For some adult dogs, a natural mineral product called K-Zyme in their food seems to help stop stool eating, but there's no guarantee because it *is* a normal canine activity. Disgusting, but normal.

Prevention: Caprophagy, or eating excrement, is natural in dogs. Not all dogs do it, but all are programmed to, maybe because this is how the mother keeps her new puppies and their den clean. Pups see her do it and some—but by no means all—may try emulating her housecleaning technique. But that, too, is conjecture. Some dogs never have the opportunity because they are always walked. The only hazard to the dog is if parasites are ingested. Have your veterinarian check the dog regularly for worms.

Question: "Our puppy was paper trained in the basement. Now she stays outside all day while we're at work, and every day as soon as we let her in, she goes! Why does she do this?"

Answer: You taught her to use papers, but probably didn't spend enough time teaching her where to go outdoors. Spend a weekend taking the dog out *on leash* to a small area you want her to use, starting first thing in the morning and continuing every hour or so all day. The dog is put on leash because you must say "Good dog" *as* your pup relieves herself. Instead of letting her into the house when you come home from work, play with her outside for a few minutes, then put on the leash and take her to the designated elimination area. Keep the dog's area outside poop-scooped.

Prevention: Having a puppy use newspapers is fine, but if Rufus is to eliminate outdoors when older, train him on leash until he catches on. It is not confusing to the dog, by the way, to be trained to use both newspapers and outdoors. If I'm going to be out all day, I leave papers by the back door. I know *I* couldn't wait all day to use a bathroom and I don't expect my dogs to have to, although I'm surprised how often they manage it. If the papers have been used, they are disposed of without comment.

Question: "I have a ten-week-old puppy that's not housebroken, and I work all day. There's no way to put up a pet gate, so I just leave the pup on a leash tied to a doorknob. So far it seems to be okay, but my daughter said this wasn't a good idea. What's your opinion?"

Answer: It is definitely *not* a good idea. The puppy could easily get caught up in the leash and hurt itself seriously (even strangle) in frantic attempts to get free. The puppy won't learn how to play with toys because they will all flip or roll out of reach, causing more stress. And of course a ten-week-old pup can't wait all day to relieve itself. Solve all these problems by investing in an exercise pen, available in pet supply stores or catalogs. They come in various sizes, shapes and heights. Put a bed or crate in one corner and newspapers on the floor in another corner. Be sure to use this canine playpen occasionally when you're home, too, so the pup won't consider it punishment.

Prevention: A dog on the end of a rope really *is* at the end of its rope. To become a pet, a companion, a guardian of the home, a dog must be treated like one of the family.

Question: "I've crate-trained several dogs over the years, but the puppy I just bought from a pet shop messes in her crate all the time even after eliminating outdoors. What can I do?"

Answer: This is perhaps the only time I'll suggest *not* using the crate. Pups are crated in pet stores, usually on grid floors to let the excrement drop through so the pup stays relatively clean and dry. They are usually exercised and played with, but there is neither the time nor the staff available to housetrain puppies, so the pups *learn* to eliminate in the crate. Changing to a solid flooring with a towel for bedding may work, but if that doesn't do it, the alternative is to confine the puppy to a small area such as an exercise pen or small room with pet gate, with a folded towel or bathmat as a bed. Step up the number of trips outside until you and the pup have worked out a schedule. Wait a couple of weeks, and reintroduce the crate for brief daytime stays. The used towel will let the pup know that the crate is now a bed.

Prevention: None. Just recognize how the problem originated.

Question: "Please help me with my five-month-old Toy Poodle. She is good sometimes about using her papers, but other times she goes in the dining room where I used to have papers when she was just a puppy. I show it to her and smack her rear with a folded newspaper, but she doesn't learn."

Answer: She *did* learn, but you changed the rules! First you put her papers in the dining room, now you don't. What's a good dog to do? No matter. Once the deed is done, it's history. Don't "show it to her" or smack her. She is *still* a puppy and will be for another year. Confine the pup whenever you can't keep both eyes on her, and scrub the dining room area with bleach or, if carpeted, a pet carpet deodorizer.

Prevention: Confinement. (That word again!) When it comes to giving a puppy "freedom" think "toddler." You wouldn't dream of letting a two-year-old baby run free in the house while you were out shopping or home soaking in a tub. Treat the puppy the same way.

Question: "We have litter-box trained our English Toy Spaniel, and the problem is she tracks kitty litter all over the apartment and it also makes a mess of her coat. We have been trying to switch her to newspapers and she won't use them! We've even been shredding newspaper and putting it in the litter box. She won't jump into the box when she sees the paper. Any ideas?"

Answer: There's a new dry litter system (called Sweet-P) that is perfect for small indoor dogs. Instead of litter, it uses specially treated granules that remain in the box, offer better footing for dogs and eliminate the coat problem you mention. A small ramp is an accessory for little dogs that won't jump in.

Prevention: Begin training as you mean to continue. Some canine habits (good or bad) can be difficult to change.

FOOD, ETC.

Question: "Is it all right to feed my Golden Retriever puppy just dry food, or should I be giving canned food also?"

Answer: You should continue to feed whatever the breeder was feeding the pup. Most breeders and veterinarians recommend combining some canned dog food with the dry.

Prevention: There are two schools of thought about feeding dry dog food, one of which is in the Answer above. The other concerns "self-feeding," where dry food is left out for the dog all day.

Two problems can result from allowing a dog constant access to food. Due to boredom or anxiety, the dog may overeat and become obese. But more often the dog becomes a finicky, nibbling eater, snacking through life. The behavioral problems are then dominance (with the dog dictating the menu) or food guarding. Poor eating habits are time consuming to change and relatively easy to prevent.

Question: "Do puppies lose their teeth?"

Answer: Yes, by about three to four months of age puppies have lost their milk or baby teeth and the permanent ones start to appear. Don't count on rewards from the Tooth Fairy, however, because most of these baby teeth fall out at mealtime and are swallowed. It's not unusual for old dogs, especially in Toy breeds, to also lose teeth. (See Chapter 7 for more on teething.)

Prevention: You can't prevent the progress of Mother Nature, but you may have to help her along. For example, if puppy teeth have not come out, they force the permanent ones to erupt inside or outside the retained teeth. Your veterinarian can easily remove the baby ones. We now know the benefits of keeping a dog's teeth clean and free of tartar using a canine toothbrush and canine toothpaste. (*Never use human dentifrice.*) Your vet can show you how to remove tartar.

BEHAVIOR = OBEDIENCE?

Question: "My mixed-breed year-old puppy has a problem! He barks nonstop if you mention the words 'Outside' or 'Go for a walk' or 'Ride.' I jerk his collar to make him stop, but he's a real barker."

Answer: Your pup's vocabulary contains "Outside," "Walk" and "Ride," so why not enlarge it by teaching "No bark"? Jerking a dog's collar will not put an end to barking, and it's probably as annoying to the dog as his barking is to you. Teach, don't punish.

Prevention: Here's a dog in charge of his destiny. The owner says the magic word "Outside," the dog barks to show ecstatic approval of the idea, and the dog goes outside. Instant success! Collar corrections don't work. Teaching does. Say "No bark" and then ignore the dog. The act of Ignoring (see pages 47 and 50) denies the dog any response to the barking. Recognize when your dog begins to call the shots and put an end to it pronto, unless, of course, you enjoy being told what to do.

Question: "I have a very hyper Lab puppy. He failed Beginners Obedience, and my patience is wearing thin this second time around. He sometimes obeys in class, occasionally in practice, but never at any other time. He's ten months old, and my instructor says he won't outgrow it. Help!"

Answer: "Hyper" is an overused word, and would seem to be redundant when applied to a Labrador! Check the dog's diet with your veterinarian first, but I'd guess the puppy is not getting enough physical exercise. Give your pup a real workout—a long brisk walk, or retrieving a ball until you can't throw it one more time. *Then* go through the Obedience exercises, for no more than a few minutes for starters. Give your pup a brief rest. Then, without warning, say "Sit" with lots of happy, even silly, praise as the dog does it.

Try feeding right before a training class, which is contrary to what trainers recommend, because it does tend to slow a dog down.

Prevention: More and more we are hearing about "hyper" dogs that are actually just normal puppies who are left alone all day without sufficient exercise or companionship. When the owner returns from work, the dog is ecstatic with eight or more hours of pent-up energy, the owner is bushed and so the dog is labeled "hyper." If you work long hours, rescue an older dog or get a nice new stuffed one from the toy store, but don't expect a puppy to conform easily to being alone all day and asleep all night.

Question: "Monami is a Bichon Frise, two years old, well-mannered except for one thing. He barks at night and keeps us awake. The only way we can get him to shut up is to let him sleep on the floor of our bedroom. There isn't room for a crate."

Answer: You've got a smart dog! Your pup gets lonely at night, so he barks and you let him sleep in your room. (Kids pull the same trick.) If there's room for the dog, there's probably room for a crate. It shouldn't be any bigger than the dog. Using a crate as the dog's bed will let all of you get a good night's sleep.

Prevention: Crate training! But if you give in once, be prepared to do so forever after (or at least until you've gone through a long retraining process).

Question: "My eight-month-old puppy won't come when she's called. Is it too late to do anything about it?"

Answer: No, it certainly isn't too late. Begin today! Sign up for Obedience classes. In the meantime, call the puppy with her name and "Come!" in a bright, cheery voice *every* time you see the puppy coming toward you. Outdoors, a leash will give you the means to be sure of success. With the puppy on a long leash, run past her, enticing her to chase, then turn, crouch down, smile, sound excited and say, "Comegooddog!" (That's one word, in case you hadn't noticed.)

Prevention: Never call "Come!" to a puppy unless you can be *certain* she will. Another never is **never** call a dog to you in order to be punished. This command could save the dog's life one day, and if discouraged by punishment, your pup will not obey the Come command.

Question: "How do you feel about playing tug-of-war with young puppies? A trainer told me it was okay, but friends say it will make my dog aggressive."

Answer: Every puppy I've ever worked with has loved the game, but it is a game, *not* war. The toy must be large enough for your hand and the dog's mouth with a large knot or space in between. Keep the toy on the floor or just above. If you hold it higher, or try to lift the dog off the floor to test jaw strength (or just to show off) you will only encourage dominant aggressive behavior. That is exactly why tug-of-war is outlawed by some trainers or breeders, but that's a problem caused by people, not dogs.

Puppies love to chase, pounce and pull a moving object. Tug-of-war played gently with a puppy will teach each of you to trust the other. One word of caution: This is not a game for a young child and puppy combo. Why? Because kids are too competitive.

Prevention: You cannot prevent a dog from using its mouth, so the best prevention against future biting accidents is to establish trust as a two-way street. Tug-of-war is another way to teach the puppy bite inhibition.

Question: "How can I stop my nine-month-old mixed breed puppy from snarling while eating if I even go near him?"

Answer: Feed your pup on your terms, not his. Hold up the dish, make him Sit-Stay and offer a small amount of the food in the palm of your hand. As the dog takes it (and probably licks your hand) say "Good dog" and repeat the exercise. If there is one snarl, growl or grab, say "No!", close your hand, stand up very tall and turn away. Ignoring does wonders for manners! Gradually, over a period of several days, put an empty dish on the floor and then put a bit of dog food *into* the dish. If you are tentative or fearful, the dog *will* snarl. Be assertive!

Prevention: Protecting food is a behavior problem most often seen in older, adopted dogs who were perhaps not too sure where their next meal was coming from. Or in dogs that have learned to bully their owners. Puppies just need to be taught good table manners, like "Sit" before being served. Place a tidbit in the dinner dish once in a while while the puppy's eating and the pup'll be pleased when you approach.

Question: "Is there any way to stop a Rottweiler (nine months old) from whining to come in the house? Whenever we let our other, older dog in, the Rottie goes nuts, yelping and whining—especially at night. We yell or whack her with a newspaper, but she comes right back. She did well in an Obedience class, but I'd like to give her back to the breeder at this point."

Answer: Several things are going wrong here. First, the dog is obedient, so it's hard to understand just why the Rottie puppy has to stay outside by herself when the family and the other dog are inside. Put the pup's Obedience training to good use in the house and enjoy each other's company. If the two dogs slept in the kitchen overnight, you'd all have peace. And if for some reason you can't put the time and work into this puppy, then by all means return her to the breeder.

Prevention: Dogs are intelligent, social animals. Teach, don't punish. *Include, don't isolate.*

Question: "One of my dogs is a neutered male (two years old) and the other is a female about to have puppies. Will the male be okay with the puppies or will he try to hurt them?"

Answer: He might like them, ignore them or try to kill them. There are too many variables to give you a definitive answer. The new mother may let the male right into the whelping box to inspect her brood, or she may attack like a tigress if he enters the room! Caution is advised, and let Mama call the shots.

Prevention: Know your own dogs, but be prepared for personality changes. Also, the pups need protection from viral, bacterial and germ warfare, which the male could bring in.

Question: "We have an English Springer Spaniel puppy. She is smart, was easily housebroken, knows most Obedience commands and is a major member of the family. *But,* she constantly chews things. She has bones and rawhides, but prefers rugs, clothes, etc. We are retired so are home all day, but she's sneaky! What are we doing wrong?"

Answer: You are doing just fine. No doubt your puppy is teething and hard bones are not the only thing she needs to chew. Take a rope toy, or knot an old towel, dampen it and then freeze it and give it to her as a toy. The hard rubber Kong toy is good for teething, as are all the soft cloth or rope toys, which will substitute nicely for your rugs or clothes. Don't leave the dog with a choice. Give the puppy her own chew toy *as* you remove the stolen item.

Prevention: Be prepared for teething pups with toys they can sink their teeth into so itchy or painful gums will be massaged. Teething begins at about two weeks of age and continues for about a year. I believe excessive adult chewing may begin by providing too many chew toys during this teething period. Don't overdo!

Question: "My four-month-old Basenji is very moody. Sometimes I can hug and kiss her and other times, when I try, she growls at me. Will she outgrow this strange behavior?"

Answer: Only if you lighten up! A Basenji is supposed to be aloof. You are intruding into her space, and the dog is telling you enough of all this hugging and kissing. Interactive play and teaching are in order, especially at this age. Try a puppy kindergarten class.

Prevention: It pays to study breed-specific temperament so you'll know what to expect. And then there are always individuals that are not typical of the breed.

Two puppies saying hello. The younger one instinctively uses submissive body language.

Question: "My Standard Poodle was housebroken *and* safe to leave alone in the house at nine months of age. Now, after four weeks, she has started digging up my indoor plants while I'm at work. She acts very guilty as soon as I open the door. What should I do?"

Answer: This is a prototype for almost every question concerning the problem behavior of a nine- to twelve-month-old puppy. When a puppy is allowed "freedom" of the house, "destruction" is as sure to follow! Confine a puppy to one safe room until it is mentally mature enough to handle freedom. Many dogs never reach that level of maturity. And that's not guilt. She's just anticipating a replay of the anger you displayed when you came home yesterday.

Prevention: Dogs are *puppies* (think "toddlers") until they are two to three years of age. Confinement offers safety and peace of mind without punishment.

Question: "We have a ten-month-old Mini-Dachshund. He sleeps on our bed or with our daughter. When he barks to go out in the morning, he wets on the nearest bed while we are putting on his collar and leash. This only started about a month ago. Spanking doesn't seem to help."

Answer: This little dog needs to sleep in a crate to bring him down to size. Put the crate in either bedroom and carry your pup outside in the morning, putting the collar and leash on as you go.

Prevention: Keep little puppies off beds! In addition to behavioral complications, a major reason is to prevent broken bones or unseen harm such as damaged growth plates in legs or hairline skull fractures.

Question: "Since I got my six-month-old Dobie, he's been confined without trouble to a hallway while I'm at work ten hours a day. Now that I've given him access to an adjoining room, he has started lifting his leg in the doorway. I've tried rubbing his nose in it, making him Sit-Stay while I yell at him and clean it up with white vinegar. He doesn't get it!"

Answer: Lucky you, that your pup can last ten hours a day at such a young age, but freedom to another room was added too soon. Back up. Back Dobie into the hall. Exercise your pup outside the minute you get home. If he has marked territory by lifting his leg, calmly (without yelling or any other comment) clean it up. White vinegar is fine; so are the many new products made for this purpose.

Prevention: Confinement! (See? I told you I'd have to repeat it over and over again!)

Question: "Why doesn't my ten-month-old Boxer bark when people come in the driveway or to the front door? He sometimes barks when we play with him, so I know he can. I don't want an attack dog, but I do want a watchdog."

Answer: In a word: Wait. Wait until he is mature and sure of himself. Begin by whispering in an alarmed voice, "Who is it?" when *you* hear someone approaching. A bark is the normal response, so say Good dog when he tries. But you might want to follow this lesson with an "Okay—Sit" to show that *you* have taken over and now the dog can relax.

Prevention: Encouraging a young puppy to bark invariably results in nuisance barking. *Good* watchdogs are selective in sounding an alarm.

Question: "I can't let my German Shepherd Dog run free because I end up chasing her for miles. She won't come when she's called, so now I put her on a chain. Do you think having her spayed or putting up fencing will stop her running away?"

Answer: Having her spayed is an excellent idea, but it won't stop her from running away. A fence will keep her home and is kinder than leaving her on a chain. And *also have her spayed.*

Prevention: A fence. A leash. Obedience training.

Question: "It doesn't matter to me, but why doesn't my Boxer (seven months old) lift his leg?"

Answer: Some male puppies lift a leg when they are barely able to stand on four. Others wait until they are about a year. A norm is around sexual maturity or at around six months of age. It's not unheard of for females to try lifting a leg, generally when they are in midlife, and older males often revert to squatting. Variety is everywhere in life!

Prevention: Nothing you can do about this one! What matters is *not how, but where.*

Question: "I have two puppies—a Bulldog and a Dachshund— and I can't keep them out of the flower beds. I've tried mothballs, or catching them in the act, but five seconds later there they are, running through the flowers again!"

Answer: Leash-train them not to step over the boundary into the flower beds. Or you could try one of the several types of electronic devices on the market that emit a sound annoying to dogs. You might have to settle for a boundary of white flags if you choose a device. Pet repellents (in your pet supply store) work, too.

Prevention: Puppies are not discriminating horticulturists. Teach your flower bed boundaries, using on-leash Obedience training to let them know where is okay and where is not.

Question: "Suddenly my puppy (nine months old) has started chewing cushions and carpets. She was crate trained and by four months was so good I could give her complete run of the house. She's been spayed and she's done well in obedience. She has loads of toys."

Answer: It's classic! You have done all the right things (spaying, obedience and crate training) and the one mistake you made was to permit a puppy the freedom to get into trouble.

Prevention: Your puppy is now an adolescent. Until the phase is over, **Confine!** (Can we print it in flashing lights?)

Question: "I made a boo-boo with my Chihuahua puppy. When we first got him, he slept in his own bed in our bedroom. One day I took him into bed with me after my husband had gone to work. Then the puppy began to cry in the night and we'd take him into our bed. Now he refuses to stay in his own bed. Where do we go from here?"

Answer: Change from dog bed to crate. The first night or two there will no doubt be some whining or fussing. Give a tap on the crate, a sharp "No!" and ***nothing more.*** Ignoring a pup's cry is the hard part, but it gives a strong message.

Prevention: If you give in to a puppy's pleas once, you'd better be firm next time or be prepared to go through a long retraining process.

Question: "Our Doberman turns on us when we're out playing. She is sweet otherwise and did well in beginners Obedience. The trainer suggested keeping a long leash on her, but she chews them up. She sneaks up behind you and gives a bite on the behind and then runs off a little way, stands and looks at you sort of angrily."

Answer: A nip on the butt is not usually meant to be nasty, but is an invitation to play. However, it's one of those natural puppy behaviors that we consider unacceptable. Increase the games that will keep the dog in front of you, such as throwing a variety of toys for her to catch—a ball, a fuzzy toy, a large stick, a Soft-Bite Floppy Disc, etc.—providing different textures for her mouth. I would guess this is a teething pup.

Prevention: None. (But if you see it coming, duck!)

Question: "We were told to hit our five-month-old Shih Tzu puppy with a leather strap for soiling in the house. There's a dog door so she can go out whenever she has to, but she has lots of accidents."

Answer: *Put the strap away* and bring back the leash and return to basic housetraining (see page 5).

Prevention: Hitting does not teach a dog acceptable behavior. Hitting only teaches a dog that you are angry, irrational and not to be trusted, and that the only way to make you stop is to show submission. When dealing with a puppy or a full-grown dog, *teaching takes precedence over punishment.* **Always.**

Question: "We got our puppy at the local dog pound and she has only one problem. She hates other dogs! She's great with people and with children, but is vicious toward other dogs."

Answer: There is probably no known basis for her preferences, since her background is no doubt a blank, but you have a better chance of success because she's still a puppy. Work with a qualified trainer or behaviorist (one on one, not in a class for now), perhaps using the Saturation method and *lavish positive reinforcement.*

Prevention: For safety's sake, be sure the puppy is properly muzzled before you begin, and do not allow anyone to use forceful or aggressive training tactics. The puppy has to learn that there is nothing to fear before she can learn to tolerate, and eventually enjoy, the company of other dogs.

He drew a circle that shut me out—
Heretic, rebel, a thing to flout.
But Love and I had the wit to win:
We drew a circle that took him in!

—Edwin Markham, *Outwitted*

2

THE ADOPTED DOG

The majority of adopted dogs come from public or private shelters. Some arrive at the shelter as strays—running loose, lacking identification, not matching any reports of missing dogs. They are picked up by canine control officers, along with reported lost dogs, are kept the number of days required by law and then euthanized or put up for adoption. The whole prior life of each of these homeless, nameless, ownerless animals is a complete blank.

The majority, however, belong to a second shelter group consisting of the drop-offs, or dogs brought to the shelter because owners can no longer keep them for any number of reasons. Most shelter staff try to glean some basic background information such as age, general health and why the dog is being dropped off. Large, well-endowed shelters, with large volunteer staffs, dig deeper to learn more details.

Another avenue of adoption is through the numerous breed rescue groups that have sprung up nationwide, sponsored by national and regional breed clubs to re-home adult dogs. These are usually dogs with known backgrounds, even known ancestry. As a rule they are temperament tested, veterinarian checked, spayed or neutered, and every attempt is made to put together the best possible match with each dog and a carefully screened adoptive family.

Some dogs, of course, are adopted from Grandma or Aunt Martha or perhaps from the next-door neighbors who are moving to a retirement community.

It's easy to see why every adopted dog comes with a broad range of behaviors, from good to awful. Because of the unknowns—why the dog cowers at the sight of a rake but not a mop, why he barks at the dishwasher, why she looks at you expectantly at nine-fifteen every night—because of all those hundreds of little things for which you'll never find answers, it is better not to try second guessing. Accept your new dog as is, and put your time and effort into modifying any existing behaviors that don't fit your scheme of things.

The reasons many dogs are given up for adoption may be categorized chronologically. A puppy under six months of age is on the block because the owner can't housebreak it; or at around one year of age when going through a difficult phase, not unlike that of the teenager with similar parental frustration; or slightly older because the animal has suddenly become aggressive. Unfortunately, this is a label used to describe almost every dog that is no longer submissive as well as those behaving like normal dogs who have been allowed to run the show. There is also the much older dog whose only defect may be diminishing vim and vigor so the animal is no longer wanted.

BONDING

No matter what the dog's age, where it came from, or what you know or don't know about it, from the minute you walk into your home the transition will go smoothly if you keep the dog on leash both indoors and out. Tie the other end of this "adoption umbilical cord" to your belt so the dog must go everywhere with you and so you will be right there to *guide, prevent and teach*. This method virtually eliminates any need to punish, so it is the quickest and most successful way to retrain a dog.

Adopted dogs make strange bedfellows, but if you must sleep with a dog on the bed, please **wait!** Wait a few months until there is a strong bond of trust and understanding between you. Until then, use a crate in your bedroom. A strange dog prowling your house at night is no safer than any other prowling stranger.

Taking an adopted dog to Obedience classes will show you how Rufus reacts to other dogs and people in a group. It will also strengthen your trust in each other and give you the tools *you'll* need to maintain your leadership.

Group harmony to a dog means being either a leader or a follower. You chose the role of leader when you took in this dog. Now you must maintain that position in the eyes of your dog so he will remain a faithful follower. Obedience training helps put the roles in place, but it's not a Marine boot camp. Make it a fun, happy learning experience for you both.

THE ABUSED DOG

If you forgive an undesirable behavior by using the worn-out excuse that the dog was previously abused, you will create an even greater problem. Dogs quickly learn how to push that "abused" button, and adoptive owners fall for it every time! The horror stories of animal abuse you read about in your newspaper, or see on television, are only newsworthy because they *are* unusual.

The kind of abuse, if any, borne by dogs that show up in animal shelters is most likely to have been verbal. Or the widespread abuse that is benign neglect—inadequate training or health care, or unrealistic expectations—which add up to irresponsible pet ownership, not the abuse one generally associates with the word, like starved, beaten, etc.

Instead of using "abuse" as a reason or an excuse for something Rufus does, try a more logical and positive approach. Assume that the dog simply has not been *taught* what *you* consider to be acceptable behavior. That is the job you took on when you adopted this dog. Wipe the slate clean by putting out of your mind what might have been and begin on day one to fill in the blanks with good teaching.

THE ADOPTED DOG: SPECIAL DOGS, SPECIAL PROBLEMS

Question: "I adopted a German Shepherd Dog. She's about three years old and in good health. She's great with me and I love her very much, but she is literally death on cats. So far she has killed my sister's cat and two of the neighbor's cats. She has never attacked a person, but she does growl if she sees children. What should I do?"

Answer: The dog's attitude toward children is bordering on dangerous behavior. All growls are warnings and need to be taken seriously. Seek professional help to work with you on retraining the dog, because it's essential to change the dog's response to one of pleasure at seeing cats or kids. In an otherwise good-natured dog, you should be successful. However, because children are unpredictable, this is a dog that should never be left alone unsupervised with a child.

Prevention: Be pushy about finding out what a dog's hangups are before adopting, not just the reason this dog is available.

Question: "We have three youngsters and want to adopt a dog. What should we be looking for? We have a fenced yard and our school conducts free Obedience classes."

Answer: Locate a dog that is really fond of kids, not just tolerant of them, and one that is the breed, or type, or size everyone in the family can agree upon. Particularly Mom, since she'll be the one to take over care of the dog when the kids are lax. And they will be. If the kids are over the age of five or six, a puppy would be a good choice. You already have two important elements for success—a fence and a teaching facility.

Prevention: In this case the Answer is the best prevention.

Question: "The Tibetan Terrier we adopted from a breeder is so scared of normal household noises—like the dishwasher, pots and pans, the mixer, etc.—we don't know what to do with her! She's six years old and a great dog otherwise."

Answer: Your dog was probably raised in a kennel, and while she was nicely socialized with people and other dogs, was not acclimated to the strange sounds of a modern home. Take advantage of her having been a kennel dog and put her in her crate with a toy and a treat before you start preparing a meal with pots, pans and mixers. When she's quiet and composed, throw her an occasional smile or a Good dog. Otherwise ignore her. Take her into another room for playtime while the dishwasher is running. She'll accept it all in time.

Prevention: Do *not* pick up a dog that is frightened and do *not* try to cajole by cuddling or murmuring sweet nothings in the dog's ear! The idea is to get the dog over the fear. Comforting only prolongs it.

Question: "Housetraining the Collie mix we adopted from the local shelter is proving to be a family problem! No one wants to clean up after him, and he urinates anywhere in the house. We walk our dog at least four times a day."

Answer: The lack of housetraining could well have been the reason he ended up in the shelter. Don't give up! First, go to your veterinarian to be sure there is no physical problem or parasites. Then go on a puppy schedule: crated or confined at night, taken out on a long leash to one area first thing in the morning. Let him lift his leg all around that one area in order to mark "his" territory. This is a very important instinctive activity for a dog, especially an adopted one, and should be allowed—but obviously only outdoors! Stay on the puppy schedule with confinement to one room unless a responsible family member can keep an eye on him to prevent leg lifting in the house.

An Adopted Family.

Walking the dog is for fun and for exercise, but it is a separate activity from basic housetraining.

Prevention: This puppy schedule should be adhered to from the moment *any* new dog sets one paw in his or her new home. A dog should not be punished for ignorance of your rules until taught what they are.

Question: "We took on Schmartz (a Miniature Schnauzer) from my uncle, who went into a nursing home. The dog is familiar with our house and was fine for a couple of weeks. Then he began to whine and pace day and night. Nothing we've done seems to stop it. Will he eventually get over whatever is wrong?"

Answer: The dog is grieving, and yes, the chances are good he will get over it. As with many stress-related behaviors, now is a good time to go for long, therapeutic walks in woods, along a lake or stream or beach—whatever you can manage that will change the dog's mental outlook. Massage grooming also helps to ease stress.

Prevention: Dogs certainly do grieve. You can't prevent it, but you can show empathy by providing physical and mental distractions.

Question: "My neighbor's company moved him overseas and we adopted his dog. About ten days later the dog began to behave in a very strange way. She barks and runs to the door. We let her out and she just stands there looking at us. We can't figure out what she wants. She was fine at first, but now she can't seem to settle down in the house. We've known the dog since she was a pup, and she's been in our house numerous times over the past two years. Have you any idea what's going on?"

Answer: It's another type of grief—homesickness. The dog is telling you that it's been a nice visit and now she'd like to go home! Since that isn't possible, increase interactive games, take her to training classes (for bonding and a little canine social activity) and also the type of walks mentioned in the previous Answer. Be cheerful but matter-of-fact in dealing with the homesick dog. Dogs can't handle commiseration.

Prevention: Physical and occupational therapy! Homesickness in dogs (separation anxiety) is not at all unusual and can't really be prevented. Knowing that it can happen and adding stimulating exercise in the form of walks and training will get the dog over it.

Question: "There are only two problems with the dog we got from the local pound. She goes crazy if we try to bathe her, and she won't eat out of a regular dog dish. It's like she's trying to snatch the food without putting her face near the dish!"

Answer: I wish I had a nickle for every dog that doesn't enjoy a shampoo, or shies from a few raindrops. Don't make a production of it. Let the dog stand on a rubber mat or bath towel in an empty tub every day for two or three minutes—no water, no shampoo. And only a happy, cheerful voice. (This is fun! Stupid, but fun!) When that much is okay, use a gentle spray attachment to wet down her legs. Towel-dry. In a week or so you'll be able to do a complete shampoo.

My guess is you have a metal feeding pan. Some dogs shy away from the glare of the metal or the clatter when it moves. Change to heavy plastic or ceramic placed on a rubber mat so the dish won't move.

Prevention: More bathing tips: Use a very gentle spray and quite warm water (a dog's normal body temperature ranges from 100 to 102 degrees). Rinsing is just as important as shampooing. You almost can't rinse too much.

Question: "When I adopted my Dalmatian, he was five months old. It was winter and I let him sleep under the covers in my bed. Over a year has gone by and I realize my mistake. What can I do now?"

Answer: Bed-break him in easy stages over a week or two. First put a towel on the end of your bed and keep him there on a long leash if need be. Next, put the same towel in a crate or dog bed elsewhere in your bedroom. Use the word "bed" each time you put your dog there while you get ready for bed. Then do *not* talk to him! Your "Good night, sweet prince" will only be translated as an invitation to crawl back in under the covers.

Prevention: Don't start! It's unhealthy to let any animal sleep under the covers with you. For starters, your combined body heat increases the production of fleas, mites, and ticks, leaving you subject to anything from fleabites to Lyme disease. It can also cause behavioral problems. Keep Rufus out of the kids' beds, too, for all the same reasons.

Question: "For three months I've been trying everything I know to help a poor abused little dog I picked up at a shelter. I lavish her with praise, treats, good food and love. All I get are growls and snarls. So far I have not been bitten, but I wouldn't put it past her. She's a Miniature Poodle (sort of), about two years old."

Answer: If you are the least bit afraid of this dog, get the help of a professional behaviorist. (Your veterinarian or local Obedience group are good sources.) If you are just resentful of the dog's lack of appreciation, try looking at this from the dog's point of view and chuck that "poor abused little dog" bit!

Growls and snarls are warning signals that say "Do whatever I want, or else!" Every time she growls and you give in to her desire of the moment, she has won another round. Take charge! Skip the attention, praise and treats for now and make this little dog *earn* a smile or kind word. Put her on an umbilical cord (leash clipped to her collar and tied to you). Get into a training class. Use the Time-out and Ignoring as needed (see pages 16, 47 and 50).

Prevention: An adopted adult dog, more than a puppy, has to be shown instantly who is in charge. Nicely, but without leaving any doubt about it. Don't weaken it with "Let's give her a few days to get used to us and her new home." (Ha! You thought I didn't know that one!)

Question: "We adopted a dog that must have spent his life on the streets. He steals every morsel of food he can find! We haven't had trouble training otherwise, but he's a thief and a good one. We seldom can catch him because he never makes a sound. Any ideas?"

Answer: Now's the time for a James Bond type of entrapment. Tattle Tale is a small battery-operated thief detector that works and cannot hurt the dog. Set it on the countertop or table near any tempting bait of your choice. The instant the dog touches the table or countertop surface, the vibration sets off the alarm. The piercing sound brings you running to reinforce with one "No!" followed by a Time-out. After your thief has been caught in the act a couple of times, the sight of the device will be enough.

Prevention: Stealing is not only unacceptable behavior, it can be dangerous, even fatal. Minimizing is not enough. It must be stopped, and the Tattle Tale gadget is good. (Can be used on furniture, plants, trash—anywhere you do *not* want Rufus to be.)

Question: "Muggs is a Boxer we got from the city dog pound, very good at home but a hellion if we take him anywhere.

He pulls, barks and jumps on people. I'm too embarrassed to take him to Obedience school, and there's no point having a trainer come to the house because Muggs is crafty. He'd be a star pupil. It's like having two dogs in one. We would like to be able to take our dog places with us."

Answer: You have one form of a canine Jekyll and Hyde. Kids often behave this way when they discover that their

"My name is Bud. I was adopted. I just passed the Canine Good Citizen test, so now my name is Bud, CGC."

parents are too embarrassed to correct them in public. Some are the reverse: "A devil at home and a dove away," as an old Scottish saying goes about kids—and perhaps dogs.

Locate a good Obedience instructor whom *you* do not find intimidating. Sit in on Beginner classes for several sessions *without* Muggs in order to learn some of the lingo, what's expected of you and of Muggs, and just to get the gist of it so you'll be more comfortable when you sign up for a first course. Explain to the instructor about the problems you're having. When you get through that first six or eight weeks, sign up for the next course. One is never enough.

Prevention: People who are embarrassed to take their dogs to a class are exactly the people who need to be there! Once the commands and the footwork are more familiar, the embarrassment fades and you'll begin to notice all the others in the class who were also embarrassed and making excuses for their dogs' behavior. To prevent problems, you need the tools with which to work. Obedience only provides the tools. The work is still up to you.

Question: "My husband adopted a puppy at the pound. It's cute, but always in the way, so I keep it tied to a doorknob in the kitchen. At night and while we're at work the dog is tied up outside. Will it outgrow being underfoot all the time?"

Answer: No, it certainly won't! At least not the way you're going about it. A puppy that's tied up all day and all night will remain an ignorant observer of life from the end of a rope. There is no other word for it—**this is ABUSE.**

All three of you need to start Obedience school ASAP. You and your husband will learn how to teach a dog, so the puppy can then learn acceptable house manners and become part of the family.

My question to you is: Why did you and your husband get this dog? For live pets that stay in one place all day and all night, you can't beat a couple of goldfish in a tank.

Prevention: All puppies are cute for a few months. A very few months. If they *learn how to learn* during that time, they will be intelligent, socially acceptable companions for the next ten or twelve years. In order to be fair to yourself and a dog, it's essential to find out exactly what your responsibilities are before acquiring the pet.

Question: "Before I can adopt a dog from our shelter, I have to sign an agreement saying that I will have it neutered. I don't think this is fair. After all, it will be *my* dog and *my* responsibility from now on."

Answer: Yes, in this day and age with pet overpopulation the concern of *everyone* involved with animals, it is a completely realistic and commendable request. (The problem of overpopulation is far worse in cats, by the way.)

Prevention: The "prevention" here is the avoidance of more unwanted dogs that will starve to death or have to be euthanized. Responsible dog ownership begins with spay/neuter, a fence, a leash, good food, good health care, good training—and that's just the beginning!

Question: "We adopted an 'almost perfect' Peke. We've had her for six months and have only one problem. She fights and screams when we try to put a collar on her. She stays right with us in the yard, but I am afraid to take her anywhere else. Do you suppose she was strangled at one time?"

Answer: No, at least not intentionally. Her reaction is more likely due to the way a Pekingese is built. The breed has no discernible neck. Skip the collar. A harness is the way to go.

Prevention: Research your breed. There are several breeds which require extreme caution when introducing a collar and leash. The Peke is one of them. Long-backed Dachshunds and Bassets are others. Or, play it safe and use a harness.

Question: "We have two French Bulldog puppies and have just rescued a six-year-old Bulldog from a breeder. She's good with the pups, but if she thinks their play is too rough, she nudges the female out of the way with her head. It's weird! The puppy doesn't seem to mind, but why do you suppose she does this?"

Answer: My guess would be that the Bulldog had previously had a litter of pups. If not, she's instinctively maternal. Using the head to separate, inspect or stimulate puppies is normal maternal canine behavior. As for why she prefers to protect the male puppy, perhaps she feels the female is too assertive and so is putting the pack in order (and setting herself up as leader). Don't interfere.

Prevention: No prevention. This mom knows what she's doing. Be ready for the pups to test her leadership at sexual maturity (around six months of age) and definitely when the pups become teenagers at nine to twelve months of age. That's when you may need to reinforce *your* leadership over all three dogs. Powers of good-natured persuasion work best.

Question: "When I inquired about adopting a dog from a breed rescue group, I was sent a bunch of forms to fill out. The questions covered everything about me, my home, my job—I couldn't believe it! I just wanted a dog, for heaven's sake, and I happen to have grown up with that breed. Do all rescue groups go this far?"

Answer: *The good ones do.* After all, they *know* their breed and to make a good match, they need to know as much as possible about anyone who would like to adopt one of their dogs.

Prevention: The need for the detailed adoption papers is to assure the breed rescue people that you can offer one of their breed the home and lifestyle that will result in a successful match—not one that will, once again, leave the dog without a home. It is hard on a dog to be a reject.

When a dog is returned over and over again, shelters refer to this as the "revolving door syndrome." It happens because most shelters do not have the time or staff to obtain accurate information on the people and often know nothing whatsoever about the dogs they are placing.

Breed rescue groups not only make the match, they offer a follow-up support system when questions or problems arise. They form the circle that takes you in.

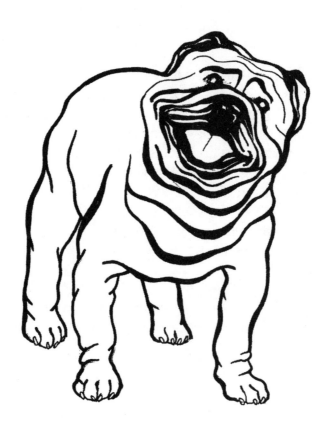

Smile!

3

AGGRESSIVE BEHAVIOR

"Aggression" is a word too often misused by pet owners to cover everything from a steady stare to a warning growl to a vicious all-out attack. What the majority of pet owners see is "assertiveness," which is a normal challenge by a dog for a larger piece of the pie. All dogs live in a society, whether ours or theirs, that is governed by strict rules of hierarchy—the order of the pack.

Dogs that are unsure of their place in the family (people and/or other pets) will challenge all those they consider to be one rung up on the ladder until they find their niche. They are great opportunists, especially through adolescence. Dogs that are babied for life remain advantage-takers for life. A dog that has not learned to trust, and to be comfortable with the pack leader, remains alert for any possible chance to advance in pack status, and, in so doing, is often considered a dominant, difficult dog—or, at times, an aggressive one.

Dogs knew all about *carpe diem* (seize the day) long before ancient Latin scholars or present-day T-shirts popularized it!

Dominance is a behavior problem only when the owner is lax or inconsistent in maintaining rules, and so cannot develop a trust relationship with the dog. Or when the owner doesn't realize that attempts at dominance by an adolescent dog are a normal stage of growth, requiring discipline—teaching, not punishing. The best owners unfailingly know when to say "Do it this way. Good dog!"

If your response is "iffy"—or even a definite maybe—Rufus will jam his foot in the door and become *more* forceful, perhaps using a warning growl or a curled lip. If that makes you back off, next he will come at you with narrowed eyes, flattened ears and a display of full dentition. Now we've turned the corner and are dealing with *dominant aggression,* which is a nasty business no matter what label we give it.

If you respond to the dog's attempts at dominance with brute force, you have stepped onto the dog's playing field. Aggressive behavior from the owner will be met by aggressive behavior from the dog. It is a fact of life that aggression feeds on aggression.

ASSERTIVENESS

Assertive behavior is most obvious during adolescence. A well-trained dog only needs a "knock it off" response to come into line. If your dog is like most pets, let's say "casually well trained," you may have to reinforce your message several times in a day, or the dog may give you a week off before trying it again, perhaps with a different approach. Consistency on your part builds the trust I keep talking about that's needed to end this nonsense.

Think just plain "dog" rather than "aggressive dog" when Rufus suddenly behaves like a canine rather than the sweet, compliant, fuzzy companion you've begun to take for granted. Get back to basics.

Reinstate routine Obedience commands (Sit, Down, Heel, Come, etc.) at odd times and for no particular reason other than the fact that you have requested it. Rufus can then relax, knowing you are still in charge. If things get out of hand, use a Time-out. (If things are way out of hand, *you'll* benefit from a Time-out, too!)

TIME-OUT

For the dog, a Time-out is a few moments of utter boredom, deprived of your company, attention, conversation, etc., that clearly indicates to the dog your displeasure. Use the crate (especially for a puppy) and the word "Time-out" instead of "Crate" and without any anger at all in your voice. (That's the hard part.) If you have no crate, any boring, relatively escape-proof spot in the house will do, such as a bathroom (remove towels and rugs), mud room (remove boots and hats) or hallway (ditto). It can be the good old sit-in-the-corner, or on a chair in the middle of the kitchen.

Holding back your anger and frustration, say "Time-out" loud and clear and train the dog initially by leading it to the spot you've selected, at which point you will have to add "Stay." Remain in the vicinity but pretend to be engrossed in something else. Do not speak. Do not look at the dog. Do not walk near the dog. Use a solemn "Okay" to release the dog—*not one more word!* Naughty Nellie is not in your good graces yet. Ignore her for a while longer to let your message sink in.

Patches got carried away with her version of "gardening," so now she's having a Time-Out.

REAL AGGRESSION

There are several causes of "nth degree" aggression that range from inherited temperament, to physical abuse, to severe illness, to excessive pain, etc. In many instances the actual cause remains unknown. There are also several types of aggression, but no matter what it's called, it generally surfaces when the dog is about one year old. Almost 70 percent of these cases are in males. Aggression is the number one reason people seek behavioral advice.

Any dog that growls, bares teeth and attacks or bites, or threatens to, is not an animal for the average pet owner to handle. Call your veterinarian or your Obedience trainer and get professional help as quickly as possible. Your own fear to correct or interact with such a dog is sufficient reason to seek professional help immediately.

Do **not** drop this dog off at a shelter for someone else to cope with. Have the dog's health, temperament and general behavior professionally evaluated. If the prognosis indicates that there cannot be a total reversal (and no excuse clauses like "if you do this" or "maybe if the dog does that") then do the caring and responsible thing and have the dog euthanized by your veterinarian. A dominant-aggressive dog that is only controlled by tranquilizers or behavior-altering drugs is a time bomb, and no one should attempt to live with a time bomb and call it a pet. There are plenty of good, loyal, steady, trustworthy, friendly dogs just waiting for the chance to be someone's best pal.

Question: "Freckles, my Cocker, has always stayed off the furniture, but lately she has started jumping into my lap when I sit down. I tried pushing her off the first time, but she curled her lip at me. Is this just old age or is it a sign of aggression? She's four years old."

Answer: Sorry, but four years doesn't qualify your Cocker for senior citizenship! And the threat of a curled lip isn't exactly what anyone wants in a lap dog! The easiest response is to stand up quickly *as* you say, "Off!" That means "no" to being on the furniture and "no" to the dog's method for trying to get around the rule. Not another word. Just walk away and *ignore the dog.*

Prevention: Obviously the dog had tried other methods for getting onto the furniture without success, so it dreamed up this one. Do not let the dog define the rules—with or without curled lip. Before you sit down, put the dog on a Sit-Stay. "Off," like all other commands, must be firm. Say it once, and if the dog doesn't comply immediately, collar the dog gently but firmly *off.* Staying one step ahead of a persistent dog takes fortitude. Being a mind-reader helps.

Question: "My dog looks guilty if he does something wrong, but when I go to punish him, he growls at me. It's scary."

Answer: Sure, it's scary. That's why he does it! But so far researchers have not been able to confirm that dogs have a conscience. What you see is not guilt. It's submission to your signs of anger—tone of voice, facial expression, body language. However, when your dog dared to challenge you with a growl—lo and behold, *you backed off!* Teach your dog things to do to win your approval so you won't have to punish. In the meantime use a Time-out instead (and stay cool).

Prevention: Utilize any Obedience training (formal or informal) and an abundance of good dog rewards in order to build confidence in your relationship. If the misdeed has already been done, it's history so far as the dog is concerned, and punishment is a waste of your time and confusing to the dog.

Question: "We have a litter of puppies and one of them is really aggressive, always picking fights with the others. Why does she do this and how should we stop it?"

Answer: One or two pups in a litter will often become bullies. It's sparring, not fighting. In other words, the pups are practicing canine survival tactics. The pretend attack, make-believe ambush, tail biting, wrestling and lots of noise are all part of growing up and learning what they need to know to be dogs.

Prevention: Separate the litter into smaller groups *only* if one pup continually picks on a specific pup, or draws blood. Work with the dominant pup gently, but firmly, using positive reinforcement and no punishment.

Question: "Our female German Shepherd is driving me crazy. She barks and growls and has even attacked my other dog. She won't let the kids in or out of the car. I yell at her and I've tried to pin her to the ground as I was shown to do, but it doesn't work. When I have to yell at the kids or my other dog, she bites me. I love her, but ...."

Answer: Your dog may have learned to bark *because* you yell! Calm down. Stop yelling! Use the Time-out when needed. You'll find it a whole lot easier than trying to wrestle a German Shepherd to the ground! In fact, that *alpha roll* exercise can actually be dangerous and counterproductive. Give the dog some fun attention when things are relatively quiet in your household. As for the kids and the car, whatever happened to "Sit-Stay" or "Wait"? (For the kids, too.)

Prevention: Increase the dog's physical exercise and *use Obedience training.* Skip the nagging and yelling.

Question: "I bought an English Springer Spaniel puppy from a breeder. The pup was sweet and adorable until about three months ago when she began to fly off the handle for no reason at all. The first time I thought she'd been stung by a bee, but this same sudden outburst has happened several times and I've been badly bitten twice."

Answer: What you describe could be what is referred to in layman's terms as "rage syndrome" and is not uncommon in Springer Spaniels. The predisposition to this form of aggression is inherited. See your veterinarian. Some dogs respond to drugs, some to behavior therapy, and some are not controllable and must be euthanized. Be sure to notify the breeder, who not only needs to know, but who may be able to help. Studies to find the cause are underway at the Cornell Animal Behavior Clinic in Ithaca, New York.

Prevention: Check out the possibility of inherited breed-specific problems in books on the breed. Then double-check with breeders to locate stock that is most healthy, but realize that there are some inherited defects in dogs, as in humans, that are not discernible before maturity. Rage syndrome is one.

Question: "We have two Sheltie pups and a five-year-old female Collie. The Collie keeps mouthing one of the pups in what I think is play, but I'm not too sure. Punishment hasn't worked on the old dog and the pup just comes back for more. Should I ignore it?"

Answer: Think of it as motherly love (doggy version).

Prevention: No need for any.

Question: "My dog was attacked by a large dog when we were out walking. Now he becomes the aggressor when we meet other dogs. How can I correct this?"

Answer: This is a tough one, because a stern correction from you could be as threatening to your dog as the imaginary canine attack he is fending off. Work with a trainer on resocializing your dog, preferably with several friendly, nonassertive dogs in more of a play situation than just an Obedience class. You may have to muzzle your dog at first for all-around safety.

Prevention: Early socialization with dogs and people is important. It is a primary reason for attending puppy kindergarten training classes. Dogs raised without the interaction of other dogs lack canine social skills. Then, when they behave inappropriately toward strange dogs, sending improper body language signals, they become victims of attack. A puppy or dog that is attacked by another dog needs to get back into the social flow by friendly persuasion, not pressure, in order to prevent further misunderstandings.

Question: "Will my dog's nasty temperament change after she's had puppies? She's just a pet, but she growls and snaps at kids, other dogs, even my friends."

Answer: I hate answering a question with a question, *but:* *Why* on earth would you want to breed a dog with such a rotten disposition? **All pets should be spayed or neutered,** *especially* nasty ones.

Prevention: People use the excuse "I didn't pick my parents," but with dogs you *can* select the parents! Spaying or neutering *sometimes* softens a dog with an attitude, but don't count on it.

Question: "This sounds stupid, but my dog attacks bicycle tires as if they were demons. She sounds vicious, but is not aggressive otherwise. How can I break her of this?"

Answer: It's a common problem. There are two causes. First, it's a moving object, which is reason enough for many dogs. Second, for the dog, the end justifies the means. After all the commotion, the bicycle either takes off in a hurry or it stops and the dog "catches" it. Either way, the dog figures she's a winner even if she has no idea what to do next with her prize.

Put some hot dog slices in your pocket. Put the dog on leash and spin the wheel of a bike on its side. Give a firm "Leave it" command and offer a treat for compliance. Repeat until the dog shows no interest in the wheel. Then have someone straddle the bike, move it back and forth and finally ride by slowly. Gradually eliminate the food rewards or the dog will be too fat to chase bikes!

Prevention: Accustom a puppy to strange moving and stationary objects early on, but avoid the fear phase, which kicks in at about five months, or wait until the pup is over it.

Question: "Our Doberman has become aggressive toward people. He was very friendly as a puppy. He's almost two years old. We keep him chained to the dog house during the day while we're at work. He can see people passing by, but now when neighbors or friends go to pet him, he attacks them. How come?"

Answer: Chaining a dog is just one way to make a dog vicious. He lunges toward the approaching person, is caught up short by the chain, receives a painful jolt and so associates people with pain. The result is a perfect example of aggression feeding on aggression. Fence the dog where it can't see people passing by but will provide more exercise. Work with a trainer on resocializing the dog.

Prevention: Fence, don't chain.

Question: "Why does my dog growl when we go to the vet's office? She is an otherwise friendly Soft Coated Wheaten Terrier. The vet has never hurt her."

Answer: She's got cold feet and is letting you (and anyone else within earshot) know that she feels threatened. Visit the vet's office as often as you possibly can, staying a few minutes, leaving and returning over and over again. (See the discussion of Saturation in Chapter 8.)

Prevention: Make the first trip to the dog's doctor a fun trip. Use an upbeat, cheery voice to transmit your sense of a good time ahead. A Sit on the floor earns a reward. Don't coddle, comfort or give the dog any more cause for anxiety.

Question: "My two-year-old Fox Terrier snarls and growls when holding a stolen object in his mouth and we try to get it back."

Answer: During a playtime, teach your dog to hold something in his mouth because *you* say so. Make him Sit facing you. Use a firm foot on a short leash to be sure the dog stays put. Hold a tube from a roll of paper towels in both hands and put it in the dog's mouth as you say "Take it." Immediately say *"Good* dog. *Give* it" or "Drop it." Smile! Do *not* tug or pull. The dog must learn to let go when you say so.

Prevention: A certain amount of "terrier talk" is normal and not meant to be threatening. Your job is to learn what is and what isn't. Teach a very young puppy to Drop It, which is more useful because it can be ordered on the run, and frankly, you won't always *want* to be given everything a pup picks up! This is another command that could save a dog's life.

Question: "My Siberian Husky was about ten weeks old, asleep on the couch. As I lifted Tiger up to put him in bed, he snapped at me. A couple of months later he was asleep on my bed and snapped and growled as I reached to move him. What's going on?"

Answer: It's that centuries-old rule: Let sleeping dogs lie. And it is still a good rule. Don't even *touch* a sleeping dog. Instead, clap your hands as you approach the snoozer, and in a friendly voice call your dog's name.

Prevention: Keep pups off furniture for safety's sake, and teach the Off command.

Question: "My eight-year-old German Shepherd Dog is now blind. Twice he has been attacked by other dogs, once when on leash and once when tied up. Now he's very aggressive on leash, but fine off leash. However, because he is blind, it isn't safe to let him off. What now?"

Answer: Being a sensible animal, he's not about to let those frightening events happen again. Now he needs a fenced area, with walks in a safe open space such as a park or field, on a retractable leash to give the feeling of freedom while you can be his eyes and guard his safety.

Prevention: Dogs that are left tied up are completely vulnerable to being teased, attacked or killed, but it's far worse for a defenseless blind or deaf dog.

Question: "Whenever my little sister tries to pick up my Shih Tzu, he bites her. He doesn't bite anyone else, but just gives her one look and then bites. Why? She has never hurt him."

Answer: The dog is maintaining a pecking order that places your younger sister below your dog. Work on changing that idea by showing her how to give routine commands (Sit, Down, etc.) in a soft voice with a big smile. Have her crouch down and call the dog to her with a visible treat or toy in her hand. And until they are making real progress along these lines, your sister must forget about trying to pick up the dog.

Prevention: Standing over a dog, or bending over it to pick it up, is seen by a dog as threatening body language. This is typically a small dog problem, since large dogs are seldom picked up.

These pups are learning by playing. It is not aggression, but rather the pups rough-and-tumble way of learning to read body language and bite inhibition.

Question: "Monty is a Labrador. Our only problem is that he growls when we put down his dinner. He turns his head as if to bite if we don't get out of the way quickly. Got a cure?"

Answer: Food guarding is unacceptable. Put Monty on a Sit-Stay about six feet from where he normally eats and make a big production of putting the dish down. Keep on the Stay for a moment more and then give him the okay. If that doesn't work on Monty, hold the dish so he can see it and take out small handfuls, offering them one at a time from the palm of your hand, fingers together. One growl and the dish goes back on the counter, you walk away and Monty can go hungry for fifteen minutes. Repeat until he catches on.

Standing over a dog that has a tendency to guard food gives him cause to do so. Keep all children out of the room when this dog is eating.

Prevention: Teach your defender of food two things: *You* giveth so *you* can taketh away. And Monty has to work for his dinner! From day one puppies should be taught that hands are allowed anywhere in or around their food. One easy way to do this (in addition to the above) is to *add* a special treat to the dish every now and then while the pup is eating.

Question: "My Akita is considered to be aggressive and the trainer told me to roll her over on her back and hold her down until she relaxed and became submissive. This presents a funny picture. I'm 5'1" and weigh ninety-four pounds. My dog is bigger than I am!"

Answer: It would be funny if it were not extremely dangerous for anyone to attempt wrestling an aggressive dog of that size and strength to the ground. Besides, giving the dog such a good chance of winning defeats the purpose. Work with a behaviorist to evaluate the extent of the dominance-aggression and to determine what, if anything, can be done about it.

Prevention: Check temperament carefully when purchasing a dog, especially a dog that will be large and strong at maturity. Positive obedience training is essential.

It seems appropriate to end this section with a reverse problem.

Question: "I bought a German Shepherd Dog to be a watchdog. He is now eight months old and is weird. He doesn't bark or growl or snap at anyone or anything. He just wags his tail and wants to be friends. What can I do to make him more aggressive?"

Answer: Your dog will be a puppy for another eighteen months. If you try "to make him more aggressive" now, in a year's time you'll be wondering why he bit the child next door, attacks other dogs, snarls when you pet him and so on. Assertiveness (the somewhat bossy dog) is okay if you like it, but a dog with a bad attitude is not acceptable.

Most dogs are watchdogs instinctively, that is, they guard territory by barking to alert the owner, or on occasion will attack an intruder. It takes little or no training on our part other than allowing a dog to be a dog and developing strong mutual trust. And that is done by consistent and fair discipline.

Prevention: There's a surfeit of aggression in the world. Teach your dog tolerance and friendliness. Canine instinct will surface to cover emergencies.

The more, the merrier!

4

MULTIPLE DOGS

Multiple dog ownership is not for everyone. We can accept that. What mystifies a lot of pet owners is the fact that not every dog craves a multiple canine family.

A fastidious housekeeper managing one dog very well might freak out at the upsets caused by the addition of a second dog. A laid-back family with four kids is more likely not to notice the extra work of two or three dogs.

But...well-meaning responsible people often take on a second dog for all the wrong reasons. For instance, a single person with one pet may decide Rufus needs a companion during the long boring workday. That's a possibility. On the other hand, Rufus may like it just fine the way it is, thank you, knowing that when the door opens each evening, and probably all weekend long, he has *his* best friend (you) all to himself.

A working person may have forgotten how long it took to train Rufus not to stare out the window and bark, or for the dog to overcome separation anxiety and tolerate being left alone. A second dog could set things back to the point where there would be *two* dogs barking, *two* dogs destroying the apartment or *two* dogs digging up the yard.

It's wishful thinking to assume a second dog will only learn *desirable* behavior from the first. Two dogs will be more active during the day (at least in the beginning) and so increase the need to relieve themselves. Newspapers? Litter box? Dog walker? Home for a walk-the-dog lunch? Even good ideas can backfire.

Those who manage multiple dog households with ease are apt to be easygoing people with low-pressure lives. Or they have had multiple dogs all their lives. Or they just put a lot of realistic thought into the acquisition of each animal.

The people who run into a wide range of problems are the self-proclaimed dog lovers who add dogs on impulse, listening to their hearts, not their heads. They may end up with five or six dogs in a range of sizes, ages and breeds, and invariably a similar span of problems. They mean well, generally "saving" or "rescuing" the animals, but this kind of multiple dog ownership too often and too easily gets out of hand, which brings us to the next point.

PEACEFUL COEXISTENCE

Dogs do not necessarily all get along under one roof. Look at it in human terms, and rather than "one big happy family," think of it as a sensitive in-law relationship. Two dogs will relate to each other more as siblings than as star-kissed lovers, regardless of their genetic makeup. Squabbles come about because they are living "under one roof." Since that roof belongs to the human, the person who is the Leader is one to be charmed, wheedled and seduced, all of which can lead to sibling rivalry, even a dog fight. It doesn't take an iron rod to maintain peace. It can be done with something as simple as a warning look or way of standing.

If you think that adding a second dog will eradicate your first dog's problems, think again! If your present dog has any behavioral defects, solve the unacceptable behavior in the dog you already have before considering another. Of course, by the time you've done that, you may decide your one (now very nice) dog deserves all your attention and you won't want to share the enjoyment! You wouldn't be the first or the last to renege on multiple dog ownership.

Still want two? Great! I admire steadfast determination, but take another look before you leap.

A MIX, OR A MATCH?

Getting a second dog of the same kind is a good choice, especially in the case of purebreds, because you will already have some knowledge of the breed. Life is apt to be more peaceful with a male and a female (neutered and spayed, of course). Ask the advice of a long-time breeder. If you opt for a rescue or any older dog, be prepared for an association that could be made in heaven—or hell. There is nothing in the Book According to Dogs that says dogs must like each other just because one human being happens to like both of them. So if it's hate at first sight, and no better at the end of a week, give up gracefully and return the second dog so it can go to a happier home.

Perhaps a puppy is what you have in mind. Regardless of mix or match of breeds (or, in fact, mixed breeds) a puppy has a far better chance of being accepted, and of accepting, the older resident dog. (It's Chapter I in that Book According to Dogs, "Honor Thy Seniors.") A pup with a stable temperament will not challenge an older dog until it reaches sexual maturity at six to twelve months, if then, giving the owner time to set the house rules and to indicate who is really running the show.

PREVENTION, OR HOW TO BEGIN

Start off as you mean to continue. That means *you* must take charge. Don't give the two dogs a few days to get settled before assuming your role. Rules are rules. It may be cute when your dog, Lulu, teaches the newcomer how to bark for a treat, but not so cute when Baby Buffo teaches Lulu how to knock over the cookie jar.

Introductions are best made on neutral turf. Let the two dogs meet in a park, a friend's driveway or fenced yard, and on loose leads. Be prepared for the sniffing, circling, sniffing, leg-lifting, squatting, sniffing, paw on shoulder, play-bow—the whole dictionary of body language with which dogs say "Hello, how are you? *Who* are you?" This ritual convention is super important. It sets the stage for the next step in their relationship.

A puppy will be submissive to an older dog, possibly rolling over on its back, eyes averted, even urinating. This is *normal* and *natural*. It doesn't mean your new puppy is a wimp. It's puppy savvy, a way of saving its own neck and making friends at the same time.

Dogs that play together stay together.

Keep the dogs confined to one room where you can keep an eye on them. And especially when you *can't*. If you must leave the house, crate both dogs for safety's sake. Without your presence, there could be a disastrous misunderstanding in the beginning, if not between the dogs, then over your possessions.

Now that we've said our howdy-dos, we'll tackle a few of the most common problems involving two or more dogs.

MULTIPLE DOGS—MULTIPLE PROBLEMS

Question: "Our four dogs were throwaways. They all got along fine until I went back to work. Someone is usually in the house, but not always. One female viciously attacked one of the others when I was gone. My vet thinks my return to work has caused this female to take over as pack leader when I'm out. How can I be sure it won't happen again when I'm not there? The dog that was attacked is a very submissive female."

Answer: I agree with your vet, and understandably, the dog who set herself up as head honcho attacked the easiest victim to overpower. You will never be able to be certain it won't happen again. Unless you have the time, money, and patience to work with a trainer, the only safe solution is to separate them when you're out, and for you to reinforce your leadership when you're home. At any sign of a conflict, use a Time-out on the dog who thinks she's your alter ego, just to remind her who is *really* in the driver's seat.

Prevention: There is virtually no way to prevent or to anticipate changes that may take place within the pack when the daily routine changes and the human leader is absent.

Question: "I have two very old dogs—ages fourteen and fifteen. The older one is deaf, and both are couch potatoes. What are your feelings about my adding a puppy? Would it be better to wait until one dog is gone, or both? I do work nine to five."

Answer: Better wait. Two such old dogs might not be pleased to have their peace destroyed by an active puppy, and the puppy also needs better company than two possibly grouchy, sedate, geriatric dogs. The only thing they might share is a need for naps. Adult dogs (eight or ten years of age) that enjoy being with other dogs would be delighted to have a pup to play with, nurture and dominate by way of teaching the newcomer the ropes.

Prevention: Consider your resident dogs from every possible angle before adding the delightful and disarming chaos that is a puppy's right.

Question: "At present I have a four-year-old Doberman and would like to get a Miniature Pinscher but I don't know if they'd get along. What can I do to be sure they won't end up fighting? The Min-Pin would live indoors and the Doberman would continue to live outside."

Answer: No dog that's been penned up outdoors for four years is going to turn into a sociable animal when you add another dog that is allowed the luxury of living indoors—with *you*! You don't mention why the Dobie is kept outside, but if it's because he has not been taught to behave in the house, you'd be wise to fix that problem before adding a second dog.

Prevention: Dogs do not understand our idea of *separate but equal*. Keeping one in and one out is just such an abstract concept.

Question: "I work, and live alone. I'm thinking of buying two puppies so they'll have company. Should I get littermates, or get one puppy now and another later? I plan to use a crate for training purposes, but will each pup need one, or can they share one crate? You can tell I'm new at this!"

Answer: Two pups acquired simultaneously, with you new at the game and at work all day, will almost certainly be double trouble. Even confined to one room, you could come home to devastation—spilled water bowls, torn-up papers, wall-to-wall you know what and chewed-up everything else! Each dog needs a separate crate, but puppies should be crated all night, not all day. Two puppies of a small breed would be safe and happy left all day in an exercise pen (that's a puppy playpen), but housetraining would still be a major hurdle.

Prevention: Why not think in terms of a slightly older dog now, perhaps a breed-rescue dog that is housebroken and not upset when left alone. Then, when you two are an established team, bring in a puppy during a vacation period when you can get in two weeks or more of dedicated training. A big gold star to you for wanting to crate-train. New you may be, but you're on the right track.

Question: "We have a five-year-old Beagle and want to get a Collie puppy. Recently, however, we found a lost dog in the park. The two got on fine, but when we got home and put the stranger on the porch, our Beagle was aggressive toward her. Would he be the same toward a Collie puppy?"

Answer: Not necessarily. With the lost/found dog, it was a case of "a stroll in the park was fine, but not in my backyard!" See how to make introductions at the beginning of this chapter. Take the puppy for an *on-leash* tour of the house, letting the Beagle tag along. Confine them to the kitchen or wherever you will be to observe how they're getting along.

Prevention: Socialize the puppy in puppy kindergarten classes.

Question: "Our two herding dogs (two and one and a half years) got along well until the younger one was about six months old. She started yelping when she ran through our electronic fence and the older female attacked her. Now anytime she yelps or coughs, we brace ourselves for a fight. Granted, there is more noise and skirmishing than real fighting. No skin has ever been broken. The younger dog rolls over on her back as soon as she can. Is there any way to stop it?"

Answer: Where there are two or more dogs, one is always dominant over the other. No big deal; it's just how canines look at life. This dominance can be so slight that the owner cannot see it, but the dogs know! Your two females matured at about the same time, but their pack order was determined when the first yelping scenario occurred. You could be causing the fire to smolder if you comfort or console the underdog.

Prevention: Give both dogs a Time-out, or if you can't manage that, a Time-out for the older dog, and ignore Poor, Put-upon, Pitiful Pearl! Have your vet check the younger dog for a possible physical cause for the yelping and coughing.

Question: "My husband and I don't have children, but we do have a two-year-old Yorkshire Terrier and, yes, he is pampered. He gets along with other dogs, but we are about to bring home a male Yorkie puppy and are concerned about how they will get along. We don't want a female because I don't want puppies or the expense of spaying, but would a female be better?"

Answer: I think Pampered Petey might take more readily to the addition of a female. Having her spayed would be a very small price to pay for years of peace and happiness, to say nothing of the health benefits of neutering both dog and bitch.

Prevention: If you insist on another male, neutering both will reduce marking territory (a major behavioral problem in Toy breeds) and may help to prevent aggressive behavior, but not necessarily. Back off on the pampering for a while before acquiring the second dog. For how to do that, see *Dogs & Kids: Parenting Tips* (Howell Book House, 1993).

Question: "I have three dogs—a male five years, a female three years, and her son who is seven months. I plan to show the puppy, who is crated while I'm at work and during the night. My problem is with the female: she eats her own and the other dogs' stool. I've tried several things the vet suggested, but nothing works."

Answer: It is normal to dogs and disgusting to us! The only guaranteed way to stop it is to change your routine so that you are outside when the dogs eliminate. After being crated all day, the puppy could do with a lot of exercise and attention, so let them all out to relieve themselves and then put the two older dogs back in the house while you stay out with the pup, playing and poop-scooping.

Prevention: The only prevention is to pick up after your dog immediately, at home or abroad. Eating excrement is more common in females, possibly due to their instinctive way of keeping the nesting area clean by ingesting the puppies' feces. That's one theory. Many abound.

Question: "My Pembroke Welsh Corgi puppy (four months old) is submissive. Okay, she's a coward! I'd like to get a Tibetan Spaniel puppy to keep her company. Do you think it would work?"

Answer: Certainly—*if* you are willing to take on the chore of raising two pups, giving equal teaching time to both. But don't do it if you are thinking to turn your cowardly Corgi into a lion, though it may improve her social skills.

Prevention: Two dogs will not each require the exact same kind or amount of attention, so long as it satisfies. One dog may be a sports enthusiast, the other a couch potato.

Question: "I am puzzled by something my two Chow Chows do. The young male wags his tail like crazy, but the older female rarely gives more than one or two wags. Am I missing something here?"

Answer: Wagging the tail is a form of communication, so the younger dog is apparently more chatty than the older one. A wagging tail is also used to indicate friendliness to the dominant dog, in this case your female. Tail wagging is a good attention-getter, too. Hey, *you* noticed!

Prevention: None.

Question: "My husband is in the armed forces, and we move around the country a lot. We have a problem with our two dogs. If we tie them up outside, they try to kill each other, and if we luck out and have a fenced yard, they go over the top. The kids would be heartbroken if we had to give them up, but it is a constant problem. Any ideas?"

Answer: Invest in a free-standing dog run (four panels of chain-link fencing, one of which has a gate). Tops are available for added safety. It can be easily dismantled and shipped right along with your furniture each time you move. Long and narrow offers a better form of exercise than square.

Prevention: A dog run is an excellent alternative to a fully fenced-in yard; the dog is free, not tied, and is safe. The free-standing run (as opposed to one set in concrete) is a good choice for people who rent or move frequently. It can even be set up in a basement or garage.

Question: "I had two cats for about five years before adopting a puppy. For a year I've been hoping they'd all get along, but the young cat will take just so much chasing, licking and play enticement, and then she slaps and hisses and hides in the closet. The older cat will have nothing to do with the dog. Is it possible to teach a dog to be tolerant of a cat? Or am I going against Mother Nature?"

Answer: From what you say, the cats and dog seem to have worked things out pretty well by themselves. Interestingly, the young cat is calling the shots. When she feels like being social, she plays with the dog, and when she's had enough, she dens up in the closet. Your dog is still a puppy. The constant need to play and to tease the kitty will subside with maturity.

Prevention: When mixing cats and dogs, it is often better to let them work out the living arrangements. Cats are clever at finding spots for a snooze where the dog can't get at them. When introducing a newcomer of either species, remember to hold the dog, *not* the cat, or you could be badly scratched.

Question: "We have a totally spoiled, overindulged four-year-old male Papillon. My wife has wanted an English Toy Spaniel and I'd like to give her a puppy for her birthday. What can we do about our admittedly spoiled brat?"

Answer: You have one enormous thing in your favor—you admit to having spoiled the Papillon! Both of you can start now to wean the dog of your constant attention (petting, chitchat, holding, smiling, cooing or whatever). Learn to ignore at least some of the cute ways the dog uses to con you into doing things for him. A couple of months should do it (see pages 16, 47 and 50).

Ignoring is a kinder solution than scolding an indulged dog for acting up when suddenly forced to share his life, his home and his people with a puppy. Your next step is to guard against totally spoiling that new puppy!

Prevention: Many problems are avoided when *dogs are raised as dogs*. After all, it's a lot easier for dogs to be dogs than to have to work constantly at being substitute children.

Question: "Could I safely bring a puppy, probably a Golden Retriever, into the lives of my Australian Shepherd and young cat? The Aussie is tolerant of the cat (only chases her now and then). He is very obedient, but my trainer felt he was becoming overly protective at around six months, so I had him neutered. He is still protective of me. Would he 'protect' me from a pup?"

Answer: You've done the right things regarding the cat, neutering and training, so I don't think you'd have a problem adding a Golden puppy. Aussies are good workers, so your dog may "work," or herd the puppy every time it moves, but a pup won't mind the extra attention.

Early socialization is important. This group has met for a run in a fenced area of the park.

Prevention: The only warning here is to watch out for more "protection" than is called for—*either* of the owner or of the new puppy. Give the Australian plenty of other work to do.

Question: "The younger of my two dogs was never socialized (my fault). She's now seven and she snaps and growls at any dog that comes near her—including my twelve-year-old dog. I'd like to get a puppy now. The pup would

be crate trained and I'd never leave the three alone together, but would it be dangerous?"

Answer: Older dogs usually do accept young puppies,
but try a controlled outdoor meeting first at the breeder's
with the puppy and your middle-aged dog on *loose* leads.
If it doesn't work out, or there's no improvement after
several tries, you may have to accept the fact that your
dog's social skills need to be improved before you can
safely bring home a puppy.

Prevention: Socializing a dog is almost as important as
feeding! Often, the problem is not due to any lack of
opportunity to meet other dogs, as in Obedience classes,
but rather to the owner's apprehension. For example,
while walking Rufus, a strange dog approaches. The
owner feels there *might* be an argument and pulls back
on the leash, giving Rufus a message that the owner is
afraid, so he reacts, inappropriately, by snapping and
snarling. He is also pulled into an inappropriate macho
body posture, being forced to uphold an image the owner
has created.

Loooooose leads!!! If you have to resort to a muzzle or
head collar, okay, but on loose leads! And get to work on
the dog's social life.

Question: "Our Poodle is great with our young children, is a
Therapy Dog and is working on her CDX. But she is a
hellion on cats! Our two have to be kept in the basement
unless Tillie is crated or outside. We are getting a Chi-
nese Crested to show in conformation. Do you think Tillie
will have the same prey orientation to the little dog as
she has toward the cats?"

Answer: All the good stuff (Obedience training, love of
kids, being a Therapy Dog) about the Poodle is people

oriented. How is she with other dogs? Let Tillie meet a Crested on neutral turf, perhaps at the breeder's kennel. Size difference is seldom a factor among dogs, but tenure on the job definitely counts! Tillie will remain top dog due to age and residency. How she handles the position—and how long she keeps it—is anyone's guess.

Prevention: Size is not a problem to dogs, but the owner can inadvertently make it a problem because it's so easy to lavish the type of attention on a tiny dog that causes jealousy, such as picking the dog up, cuddling, holding in your lap, and so forth.

Question: "It has been impossible to stop my two Beagles from picking up and eating everything they find on the ground when we're out walking. Where we live they don't have to be leashed, but when I correct one dog, the other one goes for the goodie. They are penned during the day with a self-feeder so I know they aren't hungry."

Answer: Self-feeding has some odd side effects, and constant nibbling is one of them. Switch to two meals a day and to walking the dogs on leash no matter what the local law. As soon as you've said "Leave it," put both dogs on an immediate Sit to help you maintain control of the situation.

Another hound owner had two Bassets that walked along like garbage-guzzling snow plows! We finally muzzled them because she couldn't correct the two dogs quickly enough to be effective.

Prevention: Recent studies show that self-feeding dogs results in a high degree of overweight, in addition to the development of poor eating habits. Two meals a day is the preferred way. It's always easier to teach one dog at a time what is okay and what is not okay on a walk.

Question: "We have two German Shepherd Dogs that are like night and day. The older one is gentle and sweet. The younger (three years) gives a new meaning to high-spirited! She is very strong and I can't walk her because she forges ahead nonstop. In training class she is almost perfect and she has her CDX. You figure it!"

Answer: The dog is diddling you! She can't get away with it in the structured environment of the class, so she obeys. Your corrections to the forging on walks are obviously not firm enough to eliminate the problem. GSDs like very strong leaders. Take charge! Be firm.

Prevention: The routine for an older dog does not always include adequate exercise for a second, younger dog. Increasing the activity level may be all that's necessary to improve behavior. Try a Halti head collar (a head halter) to stop the forging!

Question: "There are five dogs in our office, including my two-year-old Irish Setter. She is good friends with a Lab puppy and my other dog who is ten, but is ready to fight any of the older dogs that cross her path. Any suggestions?"

Answer: This is a group situation, and your Setter has chosen the puppy to befriend perhaps because it is *younger.* Dogs make no bones about their likes and dislikes. For safety's sake, muzzle your dog for now, and keep a crate in the office to use if she (or you or the rest of the office) should need a Time-out. Do step up Obedience training to include tolerance of other dogs for starters, with the ultimate goal of having your Irish Setter take actual pleasure in their company.

Prevention: In any normally busy office, crating the dog will relieve tension among staff and prevent a full-blown dog fight from erupting while you're on an important phone call or in a meeting down the hall. Some individual dogs are not and never will be gregarious. The best we can hope for in that case is tolerance. Fighting is not just unacceptable, it's dangerous.

Question: "First I got a cat (a stray). She was lonely, so I brought home a puppy. Then a friend needed a home for a cat and I took it. The dog and I go to an excellent training class and things are beginning to calm down a little. Should I anticipate any problems next month when I bring a rescue Greyhound into my family?"

Answer: Slow down! Wait for *complete* calm (not "beginning to calm down a little") before even thinking of adding any more pets. Better to be happy working out the wrinkles of a few animals than at your wit's end with an assorted houseful. Ex-racing Greyhounds make delightful pets, but many cannot tolerate cats because they have been trained to chase.

Prevention: It is a common mistake made by well-meaning, good-hearted people to take in more strays and to make more rescues than they have the knowledge or facilities to handle. Instead of a loving home with a few pets, they are soon running what amounts to a disorganized animal shelter. Accept your limitations gracefully and the animals will be grateful.

Question: "Our four-year-old Golden Retriever viciously attacks the eight-week-old puppy we brought home for her. The last time the puppy required stitches. We keep them separated but can't live like this forever. Help!"

Answer: Contact a trainer who can come to your home and work with you and the dogs. Until then, with one person on each dog, go for separate walks and "just happen" to meet. Let the dogs sniff, etc. (see Chapter 4) on loose leads. If the older one even marginally tolerates the puppy, continue the walk together. Separate when you get home.

Prevention: Lots of dogs don't like surprise presents.

Question: "For ten years my female Terrier mix has been the center of attention in our household. My sister lives in the apartment above us and recently adopted a very gentle, neutered adult male Collie. The two got along okay for a couple of days, but then my dog started growling and snapping when the Collie ate from her bowl, took her toys, etc. They play well outdoors, but because of his size he can be rough—and my dog is *spoiled!* Any suggestions? We love them both."

Answer: Dogs don't hide their true feelings. The Collie was nice as a visitor and is okay as an outdoor playmate, but the Terrier's home and possessions are sacred to her. Feed her when the Collie is not around, then pick up her dish. Give the Collie his own bowl of water outdoors when he visits. The Collie should be taught Drop It or Leave It when helping himself to toys. Correct your dog for growling or snapping. Now is a good time to teach the Sit-Stay if she doesn't already know it.

Prevention: Don't spoil a dog to such an extent that it can't cope with a change in lifestyle.

Question: "We had six cats and one mixed-breed dog. Then we took in a stray puppy and a Doberman. We locked the cats in a bedroom when we went out, but one day we came home to find the dogs had killed one of the cats (our favorite). The dogs were punished. Two weeks later another cat was found dead, one that was particularly

If you want a lot of dogs, it's sometimes easier when they're all the same breed (and safely fenced from the pool).

friendly with the dogs. No one has any answers for me as to why this happened, or what to do about it. Have you?"

Answer: We think of them as our pets, but a group of dogs living together consider themselves to be a pack and at any point in time may act as a pack, even attacking what one considers to be prey. What begins as a game of "chase the cat" in an instant can turn into a serious contest of animal versus animal. Punishment, after the fact and indiscriminately (since you can't know which dog did what), is completely ineffective.

Prevention: There is no training the average pet owner can do with a pack of dogs to guarantee that this would not happen again. Live a life of constant separation or look for new homes for some of these pets.

Question: "I have a well-adjusted, problem-free, outgoing English Springer Spaniel, seven years old. Where I now live she doesn't have other dogs to play with, so I'd like to get another dog. I work, and can't decide which would be my best bet—adopting a stray or getting a purebred. Also, should it be a puppy or adult?"

Answer: You have an exceptionally nice pet and you'd probably be happy sticking with the same breed. Breeders sometimes have a slightly older dog that for some minor reason will not reach stardom in the show ring, but would be easier to housetrain and quicker to adjust to your schedule. Breed clubs also have rescue services. Contact English Springer Spaniel breeders with these alternatives in mind.

Prevention: Adopting a stray satisfies the Good Samaritan in us, but is not always a wise choice. Accepting a pig-in-a-poke is not for everyone, nor for all circumstances. Breed rescue organizations offer complete and knowledgeable evaluation, plus a support system for the life of the dog.

Now you have a better idea as to why I said in the beginning of this chapter that multiple dog ownership has many facets. Not all the stories end with "and they lived happily ever after."

5

FEAR!

Face it. People do *not* admire fear. Not in ourselves, not in our kids and especially not in our dogs. We want our dogs—regardless of their size, age, breed or brawn—to be courageous.

Of course, the truth of the matter is, dogs are not all Fearless Fosdicks. Many of them have one or more fear-related hangups that range from the silly Fear of Funny Hats to the most common, which is the pervasive Terror of Thunderstorms.

Whatever form the phobia takes, there is one standard procedure the dog's owner invariably follows, and it is the wrong one. A human reaction to another's fright is to give comfort. The way we comfort our kids or each other does nothing to ease canine panic.

The cooing, comforting tone of voice and words we might use in trying to calm a child's fears have the opposite effect on a dog, serving only to reinforce the fear. It's as if you were saying to the dog, "It's okay...to be scared out of your wits.

…of people, of hats, of dogs, and
things that go bump in the night.

What a good dog…to be quivering like that! Good boy…to cringe and cower when you hear thunder!"

Great stuff, isn't it? It certainly is *not* what you are actually saying, and it is absolutely the reverse of what you mean, but that's the message your dog gets. Your cuddling may add to the message that *you* are also frightened, as young dogs huddle together when threatened.

No matter what the dog is afraid of, the easiest and least painful way to overcome it is by Saturation, which is a means of modifying the behavior by overexposure to the very thing the dog fears.

STORM WARNING!

We'll tackle thunderstorms first because they top the list of all noise fears, which includes fireworks, a car's backfire, the motorcycle's vrooooom, vacuum cleaners, slamming doors— you name it. Thunder and lightning are natural phenomena, and the dog is reacting in a "natural" way, that is, to run away and hide in order to be safe. It's self-preservation.

You can't just call up a thunderstorm in order to retrain your dog, but through public libraries and record stores you can get an audiocassette of a rip-roaring storm. There's a special audiocassette available for the prevention and treatment of all noise fears. It is called *K-9 Counterconditioning* and is available in pet supply stores. The only thing lacking will be the atmospheric pressure change, which in sensitive dogs sometimes triggers the warning of an impending storm. However, the sound alone is usually enough for training purposes.

Be sure the dog will Down reliably before you start. Begin with the volume so low you can barely hear it. Your dog will. If Barkoffsky's normal reaction is to hide, keep him on a very loose lead. Put your dog on a Down-Stay with a favorite toy or blanket (yes, that good old security ploy) in a room the dog will have access to during a real storm. Go about the preparations cheerfully, then make yourself comfortable and look at a book or magazine. Don't, whatever you do, sit and stare at the dog!

RELAX, REWARD, REINFORCE

When you notice the dog is beginning to relax, either listening to or ignoring the sound completely, calmly say "Good dog" and give a very small treat such as a bit of cheese or slice of hot dog. Like all forms of training, quit while you're ahead, when the dog is relaxed or asleep.

Still starting at the beginning of the tape (which is the quiet start of a storm), gradually increase the volume over the next few days of sessions. The instant you see any sign of agitation, turn down the volume and wait until the dog is comfortable again. Begin to eliminate the food rewards. All behavior modification takes time. The process cannot be rushed. You must only move ahead at the dog's speed. The object of this particular exercise is to modify a natural animal behavior, not just another bad habit, so be patient.

Knowing how unpredictable weather can be, you might run into a long period with nary a thunderstorm in your state, in which case an occasional dummy run or rehearsal wouldn't hurt.

There is another theory regarding Saturation to eliminate fear of thunder or fireworks, and that is to keep up a jovial, even raucus playtime. My objection to the method is that the dog is stressed out by fear to begin with, and this kind of added stimulus, even though it is meant to be play, may increase rather than subdue his anxiety. You may not always be home during a storm to be a pumped-up playmate, so I'd rather see a dog learn to relax during a storm.

Many other less dramatic fears and suggested solutions follow.

FACING FEARS

Question: "A year ago we got a Sheltie pup who gets along great with our ten-year-old Lab. We have come a long way in overcoming the Sheltie's fear of noises, but she has developed a problem with trucks. Her place in the car is on the floor in back of the driver, but when a truck passes us on the freeway, she jumps into the front seat. How can we make her stay in back?"

Answer: The first thing that comes to mind is the safety of the driver and everyone else in the car. The safest (and easiest) solution would be to use a crate, which could go in the same space behind the driver. If she has not been crated before, introduce it as a new bed in the house until she accepts it.

Prevention: The crate or car barrier or seat harness is for dogs what the child's car seat, seat belt and airbags are for people. Use them!

Question: "My neutered male dog has always been terrified of electric storms. Then he began to associate the static on TV with storms, so whenever the cable goes out, the dog hides. Next he became frightened of the remote control when I flip through channels. Now he panics if I pick up the TV guide! Reassuring him hasn't done any good. This dog used to be a nice companion for an evening, but this whole fear thing is out of control."

Answer: Keep the dog on lead and on the floor next to you and a bowl of bribery in your lap—crackers, pretzels or whatever will hold his interest. With a treat in one hand, casually turn on the TV. Reward with a soft Good dog. Flip to another channel *only if* the dog remains calm. Intersperse praise with treats. Definitely *no* "reassuring."

I can't resist adding a tricky training method. Rent a videotape on animals. Dogs or cats or horses on the screen seem to mesmerize most dogs. It may be the short-est route to regaining your TV pal.

Prevention: Sometimes dogs, like kids, behave precisely as we anticipate they will. If you are expecting panic when you reach for the TV knob, that's what you'll get. Expect the desired behavior and the results from your positive attitude may surprise you.

Question: "We own a twelve-year-old Welsh Terrier, and when-ever he hears thunder, he races around panting, whim-pering and knocking things over. What can we do to help him?"

Answer: See the beginning of this chapter.

Prevention: For dogs that do not respond to Saturation, a covered crate provides the kind of hidden safety they are looking for. Do *not* put such a dog in a closet or allow hiding there unless you're prepared for a demolition derby. Crates are for dogs, closets for people. Don't ex-pect rational behavior in a frightened, stressed-out dog.

Question: "I'm a thirtyish female with a three-year-old male German Shepherd Dog who is afraid of men. All men. He barks, growls and runs back and forth between me and any male."

Answer: Dogs do display gender preferences, but the fact that yours runs back and forth between you and men would indicate a protective behavior rather than merely a fearful one. Join a training class and work with the in-structor on socializing your dog with men and boys. Do not punish the dog in any way for trying to protect you. Just find a one-word command such as Okay, which you can use to tell the dog you are in control of the situation.

Prevention: Puppies become well-rounded adults when they've been socialized, disciplined, taught how you want them to behave and at the same time allowed to be dogs.

Question: "We live above a small shop and have to negotiate an outside staircase. Our seven-month-old Australian Cattle Dog will come *up* the stairs, but no matter what we've tried, nothing will get her to go down the stairs. We've dragged her, pushed her, yelled at her, and end up carrying this big hulk down the stairs!"

Answer: Go to the top of the stairs by yourself. Get down on your hands and knees. Now *look down.* Do you see now why puppies that are brave about going up stairs cannot be faulted for being afraid to venture down?

With the dog on leash, start training from the bottom by letting the dog go up two or three steps while you remain at ground level. Turn her around to face you and coax her down (with a food treat) very slowly. Keep her head low. Don't pull, push or drag. And do *not* let her jump. Repeat several times before adding one more step. Quit when the dog will go down half the steps. The next day, do a run-through of just that much and then go all the way to the top. Go down two steps, turn and face the dog and using your body to block the scary view of the stairs, encourage her to come down one step at a time this way until you're below the halfway point. Turn and let her do it beside you.

Prevention: This was a detailed answer because the above method is a good one to use to teach any puppy to negotiate any stairs. Puppies, like little kids, can and do fall down stairs, breaking bones or suffering head injuries. They usually figure out a way of crawling up, but for the fearless, stupid or just optimistic, the way down takes the form of a Superman leap from the top. That is what you must prevent.

Question: "Our Labrador mix was okay about riding in a pickup until one day she jumped out to follow my daughter into a store. The dog hurt her back. It was not a serious injury, but now we can't get her to ride in my pickup or even my husband's wagon. The problem is we live up in the Sierras, and if there's an emergency, I cannot lift this huge struggling dog into a vehicle. We have tried putting her on leash and using the word 'Up!' but without much success. Please help."

Answer: Dogs have a strong sense of nature's law: *Learn from Experience. Experience Is the Mighty Teacher.* In every part of the United States, dogs are bumped out of pickups, or jump out of cars and trucks on highways or in traffic and are killed, or never seen again. A crate can be anchored down in a corner of the truck bed to give a dog the safety it deserves when riding in the open.

"Car phobia" is common enough in dogs that I'll give this answer in detail. By now you'll recognize it as the Saturation process.

Install a canine seat harness in the cab of the pickup (or front or back seat of a car) and with the Up command (it's good to use a one-word command for "Get in the car, stupid") and with whatever fabulous treat or toy your dog needs, get the dog onto the seat, strap her in, get in yourself—and *go nowhere.* When she calms down even a little, give a cheerful "O-kay!" and let her out. Repeat just this much several times a day until the dog will hop right into the car (even if it's just to collect a treat).

Only then add the next step, which is to turn on the engine for a few minutes—and again *go nowhere.* With the dog now wondering what on earth you're up to, get in gear and go to the end of your driveway. No reaction? Park for a few minutes. Drive back. (Take along a book, listen to the radio or learn a foreign language.) The next step is to go a little further, only increasing the distance as the dog remains calm. When you can go a fair distance with no fear reaction, park and take your "good dog" for a fun walk.

This takes time and patience because you cannot go from step one to two to three in a given number of days. You must go back one or two steps at *every* sign of nervousness. The goal is to have the dog not simply overcome its fear of riding in the car or truck, but to make the connection of Up! with an enjoyable adventure.

Prevention: Use the above routine the first time a pup seems fearful, tense, drools or throws up, or barks in the car.

Question: "In the summer my Samoyed puppy was about five months old and he was badly frightened when a friend stopped by wearing a big hat and sunglasses. Since then he cowers and is afraid of anyone in any kind of hat or eyeglasses. What can I do to get my friendly puppy back?"

Answer: For the fear of hats and glasses, use the Saturation method.

Prevention: It's unfortunate, but not unusual, that these things happen during a puppy's normal "fear period" (around five months of age is one). During these ages, almost any unexpected thing affecting the senses is met with a response of fear. Understanding that it is a normal growth phase to be undertaken with caution, but not

Mikki is afraid of water and is frantic to get out. With gentle encouragement and the literal support of a loving owner, Mikki will overcome this fear.

alarm, helps most dog owners get through it. The dogs get through it, too.

Question: "My Cocker Spaniel is four years old and has always been afraid of people. We have just gone through six weeks of Obedience classes and the trainer says the dog is submissive, not afraid, because she doesn't hide. Instead, she rolls onto her back and urinates. I still think she does it because she's afraid."

Answer: No, it *is* submissive behavior. Submission is an important way to avoid aggression or friction between individuals in people as well as in animals. Rolling over on the back to expose the vulnerable groin and belly area is typical submissive canine body language. What you may read as fear, other dogs will fortunately understand is submission.

Prevention: Breeders: Socialize your puppies! With people and dogs. Gently, from birth.

Question: "When people come to the house my dog, McRuff, gets nervous and hides behind me, but he jumps out and nips at them if they move quickly, or get up. How can I teach him not to bite?"

Answer: This is commonly known as "fear biting." It is a form of aggression and considered to be inherited. It is a complicated behavior, and you need a professional to evaluate the dog and to work with you on the problem.

Prevention: Ethical and experienced breeders do not knowingly breed dogs with this serious temperament flaw.

Question: "My puppy is healthy, smart and well behaved, but she is terrified of people. There is no inbreeding in her pedigree and her parents are both good tempered. She was removed from the litter at five and a half weeks, and maybe that has something to do with it. I had her spayed, but I'm afraid she will develop a biting problem. Or will she outgrow it?"

Answer: Inbreeding or early removal from the litter would not cause a fear of people. She won't outgrow it without a lot of help. At home, ask people to sit down and ignore the dog. Still ignoring the dog, let *her* approach *them*. Standing over a dog and bending over to pet it are dominant postures that cause a fear reaction. Use patience, not pushiness, to help the pup overcome her problem.

Prevention: Socialize! Cultivate a puppy's natural curiosity by asking friends to sit on the floor or ground to play with the pup, using treats, smiles and calm, happy voices. Handle with care!

Question: "My German Shepherd Dog is afraid of her own shadow! This great big, sweet-tempered, obedient animal is scared to death of just about everything that moves or makes a sound or leaves a scent! What on earth can we do with her?"

Answer: You've got all those good attributes going for you and for the dog, but you don't tell me her age. This could be a normal phase, but you need a behaviorist to pinpoint the cause. One episode might provide the key to the entire problem, or it could be a major project to solve. Has your veterinarian checked the dog's vision and hearing?

Prevention: There are admittedly some things you can't foresee and therefore can't prevent. Such extreme fear in an otherwise sound dog is one of those things.

Question: "I was told that massage calms a frightened dog, but when I tried it during fireworks, my dog bit me."

Answer: Go the Saturation route (as for thunderstorms). After you've resolved the problem and the dog remains calm during outbursts such as fireworks, you can try gentle massage.

Prevention: Do *not* "reassure" or "comfort" a frightened dog.

Question: "My puppy (twelve weeks old) has a terrible fear of strangers. I don't pick her up because I know that reinforces the behavior. When she's on leash, I force her to go up to people. When she backs off, I scold her and tell her "No," and then try again, but all she does is snap and growl at them."

Answer: You are right not to pick her up, but *never* scold or punish a dog, especially a puppy, for being timid. She needs to count on you to be her trusted leader and you get mad at her when she's afraid! Enroll in a puppy training class ASAP. Meeting other pups and people, all sitting on the floor or ground, does wonders for shyness.

Prevention: Socialize!! (Can I say it often enough?) Kindergarten puppy training is an excellent way to begin. Great for owners, who also get to socialize.

Question: "I adopted a four-month-old Toy Fox Terrier who proved to be a friendly, outgoing pup. I took him everywhere, introducing family, friends and strangers. Suddenly, six weeks later, he began to run away and hide from people. What's going on?"

Answer: It's that fear phase again. (See how normal it is?) Bear with it by being your cheery self. Ignore the signs of fear and *don't force the pup* in any way, and you'll both come through it nicely.

Prevention: Be aware, that's all. Don't panic and don't force the dog to do anything until the phase passes. Each individual pup matures at his or her own pace.

Question: "We have a whopper of a problem! During a thunderstorm, our dog clawed through a wall *and* through a two-by-four! To state the obvious: We were not at home. She seems to want to get into a dark place to hide and figures on digging her way to the center of the earth! What can we do about storms that occur when we are at work? We don't have a cellar or garage."

Answer: Use the audiotape/Saturation method (described in Chapter 5) and settle her in a place she has access to when you're not home such as a covered crate with the door left open. Do you have a neighbor or a pet sitter—or a friendly dog trainer—who could stop by when a storm is approaching?

This is fear carried to the extreme and to modify it *may* at first require tranquilizers if your veterinarian recommends them in addition to the assistance of a professional behaviorist on the scene. No matter what route is taken to modify the anxiety, as the dog's owners, *you* must participate in order to understand what's going on.

Prevention: Be alert to any sign of stress and work on alleviating it immediately. Destructive behavior is the end result of several forms of stress.

Question: "Our Boston Terrier is petrified of brown paper bags. We have no idea how or when it started, but she turns to jelly when I bring home the groceries. I have to put her in another room while I unpack the bags and put them away. It's not life threatening, but it sure is annoying."

Answer: This kind of fear is often overcome just by a change of association. In this case, make a paper bag into a toy. Put a ball (the kind with a bell inside) into a small brown paper bag. Tie a long string around the top and you've got an irresistible (we hope) toy to pull along the ground. Let her watch you assemble it, and make a lot of the tinkling ball; play down the bag itself.

Prevention: We can't prevent everything!

Save your breath to cool your porridge!

6

BARKING

Barking is just one item on the list of things that all dogs do. *How* they do it we know, but *why* they do it, *when* they do it or *where* they do it is sometimes a mystery but sooner or later becomes a concern of almost every dog owner. While you may complain about barking, it's reasonable to suggest that if you were expecting quacks, you'd have bought a duck!

Recent studies of barking dogs indicate that domesticated dogs kept as pets bark more than their counterparts in the wild because they are trapped for life in a state of adolescence. It is well documented, for example, that *young* foxes and coyotes bark about as much as pet pups do, but the adults rarely bark at all. Whereas adult domesticated dogs all too often become excessive barkers, barking repetitively for hours on end and for no apparent reason. That's the idiopathic nightime barking that launches our neighbors into outer space!

A dog's bark is not necessarily cause for alarm, unless you happen to think a falling leaf or passing car warrants a police investigation. Domesticated dogs bark for various nonreasons with little or no common cause. Although it has long been assumed to be a form of communication, barking may not serve any useful purpose other than as a vocal challenge by the watchdog, or as an attention-getter from the young pup or spoiled dog.

Therefore, it is generally agreed that meaningless barking is a puppy activity carried over into adulthood along with other adolescent characteristics that keep domesticated dogs in a perpetual state of attention-seeking immaturity, a state encouraged by pet owners—unwittingly or purposefully. By the time the owner complains about it, or seeks help to correct it, barking has become a well-established habit.

There are three kinds of nuisance barking that are most annoying to dog owners.

1. The dog continues to bark after guests are greeted, or after the passerby has long since gone.
2. The dog barks to ask for everything—to go out, to come in, for treats, to play, etc.
3. The dog barks all night, or all day, or both.

Once nuisance barking has become a habit, it's as hard to break as smoking. Some dogs quit more readily than others, but it's never easy. Since we know that annoying barking, excessive or not, is a habit, it's time to stop it when it begins, not a year or two later when neighbors are tearing their hair out over the ruckus and the dog has a full-blown addiction. By the time your landlord is threatening to terminate your lease, and your neighbors have long since run out of sympathy, or you are being hit with a civil suit for disturbing the peace, *you* have a *problem!*

EXCESSIVE BARKING—THE OWNER'S SIDE

Let's look at excessive barking from a pet owner's viewpoint and come to a somewhat empirical conclusion.

The dog that sleeps at the foot of your bed, or in a crate or bed in the kitchen, does *not* bark all night. Whereas the dog that is tied up, or is kept outside, is the one that drives everyone, neighbors and owners alike, ballistic, right?

That answers part of the When?, Why? and Where?, doesn't it? Dogs are social animals, and domesticated or wild, they are not happy when forced to live alone. Dogs bark for hours on end when they are shut out of the "pack," in this case their family. We can only guess, but such a dog might even be afraid of the dark (again, the immaturity angle). The dog may bark for any other capricious reason—from falling leaves to flying bats, or may just be lonely. Tied-up dogs are instinctively aware of being completely vulnerable to any predator, real or imagined, so they bark. That's stress, and it can lead in turn to aggression.

The good news is that dogs can be retrained. Bring the outside dog in at night or, better yet, don't leave your dog out in the first place. A dog that barks, but must be left outside while the family is at work, can be intensively retrained during a vacation and on weekends. It is a difficult habit to break because most of the time no one is around to teach an acceptable alternative.

Punishing a wrong without teaching a right is a waste of time and energy.

RETRAINING

One way to stop unwanted barking in the house is to *teach the dog to bark on command.* "Bark! Good dog." After the dog has that down pat, use No Bark or Okay when you want to tell the dog to quit, that you are taking over. "Okay!" followed by "Good dog" and a *big* smile of approval the instant the barking stops.

Here's another trick that works well for the dog that overbarks a welcome to visitors. As you go to the door, pick up a toy kept especially for this purpose and no other. It should be large, soft and without a squeaky. Put Barkus on a Sit-Stay, followed by a Take It or Hold It and a quiet Good dog. This ploy works so well, many dogs rush to get their toy the minute the doorbell rings! But it takes both time and patience on the part of the owner, as with any training, to replace bad habits with desirable ones.

OTHER SOLUTIONS

One electronic device I like is called Pet Agree. The trainer has to be around because this is an attention-getting sound that only the dog can hear, and it must be followed by an appropriate command such as Come or No Bark or whatever you are working on. It gets the dog's attention and then it's over to you. A dog of mine who was a barker, and also did not always come when she was called, quickly responded to the Pet Agree and Come, which automatically stopped the barking. A "two-fer" remedy!

The ultimate cure people ask about is surgical de-barking, or the final barking solution. Think it through carefully. Realize up front that the dog will *not* be silent. In fact, the sound is not even predictable and may be more irritating to the human ear than the former barking. **Discuss the procedure and all possible results at great length with your veterinarian.** Think about it long and hard because it is irreversible surgery. Then think about it some more. You can tell I'm not in favor of this recourse.

Question: "My two-year-old Collie is a great dog except that he barks. He did well in Obedience classes and never barked in class, but he barks everywhere else when there are people involved such as meeting friends on the street, or at home. He does *not* bark at all when he's alone with me except if I'm on the phone. He gets plenty of exercise. What's the problem?"

Answer: Your dog wants you and your attention all the time, so he only barks when you are distracted. Right now, the dog is calling the shots, so let's reverse it. Catch him when he's barking (pick up the phone!) and teach the commands Bark and No Bark. I know, it's sort of your basic stupid pet trick. One bark, one treat, one praise, followed by "Okay." It will take time, but it shouldn't be hard to retrain such a smart dog.

Prevention: This is more of a tip than a prevention. Never tell a dog-in-training "Bark" unless you have a goody in one hand. Never say "No bark" or "Okay" if a dog is in the middle of a barking frenzy. You must be able to control the situation.

Question: "I have two dogs. The younger female is an obnoxious barker, even waking me up in the middle of the night."

Answer: See the previous answer, and the suggestions for nighttime barking. You haven't told me where the dog sleeps, but if it's outside, bring her in. If this is an indoor dog give her additional exercise in late afternoon or evening.

Prevention: Catch this young barker quickly before the idea spreads to the older dog! Females tend to be vocally dominant, whereas males may go the physical route. So what else is new?

Question: "Our adopted Pomeranian is well mannered except that when in the car or walking on the street she barks at people. We have taken her to Obedience classes, but the trainer said we should learn to live with it. Is that right?"

Shelties are known barkers, but Obedience training helps this owner control Jake's bark.

Answer: Perhaps the barking problem is why she was up for adoption. Use the Saturation method by having friends continuously walk by the car as you sit in the car making corrections. If the dog is loose in the car, get a seat belt (or car seat made for small dogs) so you have control of the dog. Then work on the barking. Be quick and generous with your good dog praise for every split second of silence.

Prevention: Treat an adopted dog like a puppy: don't let her do anything more than *once* that you don't want done again. If you're really on your toes, you can even *prevent* that *once.*

Question: "Our Great Pyrenees is three years old and a barker, but never when we are home. According to neighbors, the dog barks the whole day long while my husband and I are at work. She has a dog door, so can go in and out whenever she pleases. What can I do?"

Answer: Work with a behaviorist who will come to your house. You will pretend to go to work as usual so the behaviorist can pinpoint precisely when and why the barking begins in order to modify it. Obsessive barking is little more than a bad habit run amok, but you need professional help to get back on track.

Prevention: The time to teach a dog about the family's comings and goings is the day the dog joins the family. Most of us lead changing lives, and at some point the dog will have to be left alone all day. (See the discussion of separation in Chapter 8. However, most pets prefer consistency, so their attitude toward our lifestyle changes can be unpredictable. *Plus ça change....*

Question: "I have a fantastic Border Collie. She is two years old and is everything I want in a dog—except we got her to be a watchdog, and that's just what she does: She *watches!* Anyone can come onto our property. She has barked a couple of times when cars have stopped way down the road at night."

Answer: You see? Just when I think all pet owners want their dogs to *stop* barking along comes the opposite complaint! The problem here is asking a specific breed of dog to behave in a way that is alien to the breed. Border Collies are herding dogs, and since barking would upset the livestock, they are bred and trained to work in silence. No doubt the dog will prove to be a good watchdog and guardian of your property as she matures. She just won't be a barker. Count your blessings!

Prevention: Look into all aspects of a breed to be sure that the years (sometimes centuries) of selective breeding to produce certain desirable traits are the traits you understand and can live with. The Finnish Spitz, for example, is noted for its barking proclivity.

Question: "My four-month-old West Highland White Terrier is vocal about everything. It's a high-pitched bark that is almost deafening. The more I shout at her to stop, the more she barks. Will she outgrow this?"

Answer: Sounds like you're having a "bark-in" with the dog. The way the puppy sees it, she barks and you bark back. Typical puppy stuff. Take action now, because she definitely will *not just outgrow* it. With such a young puppy (and a tenacious terrier!) get her to hold a large soft toy. And if that doesn't slow her down, use a Time-out! Barking is a means of dominance, so this is a time for discipline, *not* games.

Prevention: Begin as you mean to continue. One "No Bark" command and that's it. The next bark earns a Time-out. And *no* chitchat! (that's my command to you!).

Question: "I have a year-old female German Shepherd. I live in an apartment house, and if she hears anyone in the hallway, she barks and growls, but if someone rings the doorbell, she hides under the bed! If that person comes in, and we try to get her to make friends, she quivers and shakes. How can I make her friendly with guests and aggressive toward intruders or strangers?"

Answer: You're asking too much of a young dog. At one year, she can't be everything you want. She's doing an excellent job in barking and growling when she hears someone outside, so tell her so. Let her meet your friends at her own pace. *Forcing the dog will make the situation worse.* Arm your friends with treats to be used as rewards *only* when the dog approaches them on her own, but not as bribery to get her to do so.

Prevention: Socialize puppies, but also remember that fully grown is not fully matured. Large breeds take about three years to mature. By building trust, when a puppy becomes an adult, the dog will naturally pick up your vibes of fear and tension and become a good watchdog. Just don't push a pup or young dog to do more than can comfortably be handled.

Question: "We *really* have a problem. Every night the dog barks nonstop. We holler at her, which helps sometimes. We have tried getting up in the middle of the night to go out and whip her. That helped, but only for a little while. Where she's kept in the backyard, it's dark at night and no one in the family wants to go out there. A friend suggested shooting at her with BBs. What about muzzling her at night?"

Answer: The reason the things you tried worked for a while is because the dog accepted your hollering and whipping as a response offering some human contact.

This is why so many dogs learn to tolerate abuse—because attention of any sort, even whipping, is better than no attention at all.

The solution is simple: **Stop the abuse.** Bring the dog indoors at night. Put her in the kitchen with some form of bedding (a folded blanket or a fancy new bed), a bowl of water and a few dog biscuits. For the first few nights leave a nightlight on, or a radio turned very, very low with calm music. Or both.

Prevention: If everyone in the family is afraid to go into the yard at night, I'd imagine the poor dog feels the same way. Even zoo animals are brought in at night! **This dog is not being bad. She is shouting HELP!** loud and clear.

Question: "We have a Cairn Terrier, two and a half years old. She is very well behaved, but out of the blue she started barking like crazy every time we pull a window shade up or down. However did she learn this trick and how do we put an end to it?"

Answer: The scenario probably went something like this: A shade snapped up while you were out; the dog barked at it; the shade stayed put; the dog assumed her barking was what made it stay! (Well, it *could* have gone something like that!)

Use the Saturation process. With someone monitoring the dog on a Sit-Stay (and a hand over the muzzle if necessary at first to enforce a No Bark), slowly raise and lower the shade over and over and over again until the dog does not show any interest in the activity and there are more Good Dogs than No Barks. Be super careful not to let the shade get away from you during training!

Prevention: There are some things dogs teach themselves when they have to cope with a new situation on their own. There is no way to prevent them, but they are easy to eliminate *if the retraining begins promptly.*

Question: "Our puppy barks ferociously when we're playing with her. This is okay, but she ends up biting. We've tried hitting her (with and without a newspaper), shouting, scolding, but nothing works."

Answer: The pup may be getting overexcited by the type of play activities. Try calmer, less noisy games and give the pup and yourselves a Time-out if she gets carried away. After *one* "No bark!" put her in her crate, using the words "Time-out," with no further conversation. Let her out after a few minutes, but only while she is quiet. When you open the crate door, ignore the dog for several minutes in order to reinforce your desire for peace.

Prevention: Use the Time-out and Ignoring anytime the dog doesn't respond to "No."

Question: "I have a mixed-breed that I rescued from the freeway. She's a neat dog, but she stands at the living room window and barks whenever I leave the house. If I tell her not to bark as I'm walking away from the house, she just gets all excited and barks even more. What do I do with this one?"

Answer: Confine the dog to one room, or part of one room, where she can't see you leave. Don't say anything as you leave! Parting is not sweet sorrow, and the less said about it, the better (see Chapter 8).

Prevention: An adopted dog needs to be retrained as if he or she were a young pup. Confinement is essential until all the quirky kinks are ironed out. Separation anxiety is very common in adopted dogs—for the most part with good reason!

Question: "Our dog's whining has gotten so bad that we are considering giving him away, even though we love him dearly apart from the whining at everything and anything.

I swear if a burglar broke into the house, our dog would whine the thief to death! What on earth can we do?"

Answer: Have your vet examine the dog to be certain he's physically fit. Then give the dog as much additional exercise as you can manage. Whining or barking are sometimes the result of inertia. Teach the dog anything that you can give praise for such, as Sit, Catch and Roll Over. Then *every* time the dog whines, frown and say "No!" followed by a smiling "Sit" (or whatever) and "Good dog!" Whining is a great way to get attention. Negative attention, but attention all the same.

Prevention: Don't be namby-pamby about discipline. Stop all unacceptable behavior dead in its tracks. In the beginning, the cure would have been one whine followed by a Time-out, and a release without comment only when there's silence. Or by Ignoring. Ignoring, by the way, is *not* an exercise in which you do not pay attention to Grabber. It is a purposeful discipline used to teach Grabber he cannot access your attention on demand.

Question: "I am physically disabled and have a Pomeranian who barks constantly. She is driving the neighbors and me up a wall. We live in a small town and there are no trainers nearby. Can you suggest something other than de-barking?"

Answer: First, I'd suggest you ask your veterinarian for the name of an experienced breeder or trainer who could come to your home and work with you. (Dedicated dog people will travel.) The Pet Agree device mentioned previously might be the answer (with the dog on lead) as a distraction to get her attention, followed by a command to do something positive. (Catch a toy?)

Or, the old standby that I call the "stop-it can," which consists of a few pebbles in an empty soda or small juice can tossed onto the floor every time she barks as you say "No bark." Obviously, do not throw the can *at* the dog. You want it to crash beside or behind her as a distraction so you have a split second to get in a Good dog. Attach a string to the top of the can to reclaim it easily. Timing is most important if the correction is to be effective, and if you can't manage it, do try to get someone to help.

Prevention: Stop it when it starts! Toy breeds are known to be barkers. These tiny dogs were bred just to be petted and babied, which supports the theory of the domesticated dog's lifetime stuck in adolescence with which we began this chapter.

Don't talk with your mouth full.

7

MOUTHING, CHEWING AND BITING

It's a shame to have to keep harping on one theme, but the next three canine occupations—mouthing, chewing and biting—are again perfectly normal activities for dogs, especially puppies. But beyond the age of six to eight weeks, we may find them undesirable, unacceptable, totally intolerable or even frightening, depending on the extent to which the behavior has burgeoned. For example, mouthing becomes annoying, chewing becomes expensively destructive and biting hurts!

Chewing on a rawhide or other dog toy is okay, but when a few tufts of your carpet get caught up in the process, chewing becomes "destructive" because the pup has invaded *your* turf. To the dog, it's all one and the same.

Mouthing and biting undergo the same metamorphosis. A puppy owner at first considers mouthing to be a sort of hand holding, but enough is enough, and it's no longer cute to be held hostage by a slobbery mouth. (It's yucky!) Hand holding enforced by teeth is biting.

Puppies lick their elders around the mouth as a greeting and as a request for food, making it an important bid for attention. (Survival again.) People who interpret it as kissing and encourage it are stuck forevermore with a dog that licks. Licking often precedes what the indulgent owner, who is on a kissy-kissy kick, then calls love bites. To anyone else on the receiving end of such a nip, they are just plain dog bites. Regardless of the label, the purpose is to make you pay attention.

THE DOG'S-EYE VIEW

Mouthing and biting are puppy activities that require human intervention. We may prefer our pets to retain certain infantile characteristics, but bites by any name should not be among them!

Puppies bite to test the waters, to find out how hard they can bite down before reaching the limit of the person, another pup or an inanimate object. Puppies must learn to inhibit their bites, and they learn this by the reaction they get from another dog or a person:

- Deprivation (squeal and run, or shriek and walk away).
- Retaliation (bite back, or hit).
- Submission (roll over, or back off).

A pup bites a person's hand and the person screams and walks away; the pup learns that the bite was too hard (any bite on human flesh harder than it takes to burst a bubble is *too* hard). The same pup bites an inanimate toy given as an alternative and learns to bite as hard as he pleases. No screams. No walking away. No retaliation.

A good mother takes a firm hand (or in this case, mouth) in disciplining her puppy.

Dogs also must use their mouths because they obviously can't hold anything in their paws, but this is a means of carrying and should be with what's aptly called a "gentle" or "soft" mouth.

These are just some basic explanations of how dogs use their mouths, and why, through our mishandling of these activities, our dogs get into trouble for normal canine behavior.

One basic Prevention in regard to dog bites is to be sure your dog's rabies shot is current. Rabies is a fatal disease, but easily preventable with one shot every three years.

Question: "My dog is such a destructive chewer that I had to crate-train her. If I just went to the store for half an hour, she'd wreck chairs and rugs. I didn't know what else to do."

Answer: This type of destructive chewing is typical of separation anxiety (see Chapter 8). *Never* feel guilty and never apologize for crate training your dog. Now that you come home to a happy reunion with a Good dog, life is better for both of you.

Prevention: Crate-train the pup the day you acquire her—before any destructive chewing takes place.

Question: "I give my dog loads of chew toys—they're all over the house! The other day I came home to find he had chewed (or dug) holes in two sofa seat cushions. This dog has never done anything like that before. I punished him, but how can I be sure it won't happen again?"

Answer: I guarantee you it will happen again if you leave chew toys "all over the house." This is a common complaint and the scenario is always the same. The dog is either chewing a toy on the sofa and it slips down behind the cushion, or there may be one buried beneath the cushion from some previous time. Either way, when the dog tries to get at the treasure, the kapok flies!

A similar catastrophe occurs when the dog is happily chewing on a toy and his tooth picks up a few threads of upholstery fabric or carpet. That's all it takes to begin irreparable damage. This is *not* a punishable offense. Expensive maybe, but the dog should not be punished for chewing on toys *you* provided, in rooms to which *you* gave access.

Prevention: Chew toys are great, and some dogs may even prefer rawhides to dinner, but keep them in rooms without carpets or upholstered furniture, chair pads, etc., and limit the quantity at any given time. It's normal for dogs to chew, but you don't have to encourage excess.

Question: "When I throw a tennis ball for my Labrador Retriever, she'll run and fetch it, but won't give it back. She growls, or drops the ball and then bites my hand when I reach for it. This is a dog that graduated at the head of her Obedience class."

Answer: The dog has taken control of the game. A tennis ball is difficult to remove from a Labrador's mouth (growling or not). You'll note that the Obedience dumbbell has "handles" that stick out on each side of the dog's mouth—for easy removal. Throw a large toy, or even a strong stick, as you tell her "Get it" (or whatever word you use). Keep control of this game setup by letting her see (and smell) a piece of hot dog in your hand. Say "Give it" as you put out your other hand to take the toy or stick. She is obviously a smart dog, so she'll take the hot dog in exchange, at which point you add the essential "Good dog, *good* give-it."

Prevention: Maintain control no matter what you are teaching a dog. Don't get yourself caught up in that kids' game of "Yes-you-will, no-I-won't," the doggie version of which in this case is "Give-it-back, No-I-growl-won't." You'll lose every time because eventually the growl will be just fierce enough to make you back off.

Question: "My dog and I are great pals. We do everything together. A few months ago I changed jobs and now am gone from nine to five three days a week. The dog has gone on a 'logging expedition,' chewing on every bit of wood in the house. He never did this before. He has loads of toys."

Answer: It's separation anxiety caused by the fact that you and the dog have been, as you say, inseparable and now you are leaving him behind. Toys alone can't relieve acute stress. Confine the dog to one room that's as dogproof as you can make it and put a chew repellent on exposed wood. (Judging by the number of these products on the market, it's a pretty common problem.) Leave a radio on low. By all means, teach the dog that it's okay for you to come and go alone. (See Chapter 8.)

Prevention: Spoiling is okay up to a point. A dog that is spoiled by too much attention—pats, smiles, eye contact, chitchat or, as in this case, the owner's constant presence—is a prime candidate for separation anxiety when anything changes. Teaching a dog that your comings and goings (alone) are not causes for panic ranks right up there with housetraining and bite inhibition.

Question: "What do you suggest for dogs that never stop chewing? I have two puppies (a Rottie ten months old and a Labrador four months old), and I don't know which one is worse. They chew nonstop and I'm afraid they are going to transfer this activity to my rugs!"

Answer: Puppies up to about two years of age may be constant chewers because they are teething, or simply because it's an enjoyable, somewhat mindless, occupation. Like sitting in a rocking chair. Excessive chewing can be the result of too little physical activity. Give these dogs (especially the Rottweiler) a good physical workout to help curtail their chewing fetish. And be sure they've been taught not to bite.

Prevention: For teething puppies, offer chew toys in a variety of textures—rawhides, hard rubber toys like the Kong, and large soft toys (dampened and chilled)—but only when the dog is in a crate (best place) or confined to one "safe" room such as the kitchen (second best) or the dog's own bed (third best). *Not* all over the house, because those adorable puppies (until at least two years of age) should not *be* "all over the house" without supervision. Don't relax your house rules and then blame the pup for what is normal puppy behavior. Prevent!

Question: "My Husky puppy has a habit of biting. If I walk by, she bites at my feet, legs or hands. Also, she has a nervous habit of walking around the yard making biting motions in the air. I've had other Huskies, but not one like this. She is intelligent and has learned a lot of things, but I'm constantly saying "No" to the biting. I was told to spank the dog for it. She weighs fifty pounds, and has a thick coat, so what good would that do!"

Answer: Biting, whether it's your hands, feet or legs, is totally unacceptable behavior, but biting at thin air is thought to be a symptom of a mild form of epilepsy. Check with your veterinarian or nearest veterinary medical center.

Let the puppy get a good taste of some Grannick's Bitter Apple on the backs of your hands *as* you say (firmly, with a big scowl) "No bite!" Immediately offer a toy as a substitute and ignore, don't play with, the pup.

Biting on the ankles, feet or legs can sometimes be stopped by kicking back as the dog is about to grab. Obviously this should not be a hard kick, and don't attempt it if you're not reasonably athletic or you'll land on your face! The idea is to have the pup make a connection between biting and getting bopped in the chin, so that the game is no longer fun, but the bopping had nothing to do with you. You can just pretend it was accidental—"Oops!"—and walk on.

Prevention: Puppies can be very mouthy, but biting is easily stopped when the reaction is immediate, unpleasant and is followed by Ignoring (see page 16, 47 and 50). Half-hearted "No" corrections won't do it. Mouthing is an infantile holdover in the mature dog and is generally only an annoyance, but biting behavior in older dogs should be taken seriously. Seek the help of a qualified trainer or behaviorist if you cannot quickly and completely stop it.

Question: "My dog is ten months old, and if I go to pet her, she bites at my hand (not hard, just sort of grabs at my hand) and when I tell her no, she backs off a few feet and barks—with her tail wagging. What should I make of this performance?"

Answer: The name of the game is "Gotcha." This is not malicious or aggressive behavior. It's an invitation to play from a teenage pup, so there's no need to punish. Instead, make her work for attention. Stand up tall, show your authority and have her sit or roll over before being petted.

Prevention: This is a common game, and generally used by bitches, since part of their dominance role is expressed vocally. Who says dogs don't have a sense of humor!

Question: "Sometimes when I'm playing with Bonkers, my Boxer, he bites my hand instead of the toy I'm holding. Why does he bite me when all I'm trying to do is play?"

Answer: You may have a bloody gash if you instinctively pull away, but it is really an accident. If it happens *every* time you play, and with *every* kind of toy, then it indicates aggressive dominance behavior requiring professional help. But generally this happens, especially with kids, with no intent on the dog's part to bite. Use the "scream and ignore" technique described previously to teach Bonkers to be more careful.

Prevention: Think *big* when buying dog toys. The dog can only know where the toy ends and your hand begins if he is taught to be careful. Until this is learned, give yourself the benefit of the doubt by offering more toy than hand.

Question: "My friend's dog bites people and chews on clothes and furniture, but every time I suggest some Obedience training, he says the dog is just stupid and he doesn't want to spend money on classes. I find this attitude frustrating, but what can I do?"

Answer: Absolutely nothing. If your friend would rather spend money on furniture repairs and clothing replacements—to say nothing of a legal settlement when the dog gets serious about biting—there really is nothing at all you can do. (On the other hand, you definitely have my okay to keep nagging!)

Prevention: Breeders take note. The truth is, Obedience training is for the dogs' owners. Dogs can get along without it—about the same way kids can get along without school - **not!** Shelters that offer training classes for their adopted dogs for a small donation, or even sometimes free, do a great service to owners, dogs *and* the community. Sad to say, there are always holdouts who think they know better.

Question: "What's the difference between mouthing and biting? My brother says his dog is just mouthing, but it hurts and leaves bruises! I say it's biting!"

Answer: If it hurts, it *is* biting. The term "mouthing" is generally used to mean slobbering or licking and possibly goes so far as to refer to the use of teeth to hold a hand or arm very, very gently. If the result is a bruise from a pinch or a blow from a large tooth, it's time to do some serious teaching. If there's broken skin and blood and the mouth did it, it's not mouthing.

Prevention: On the theory that if I say it often enough, another person out there will catch on, here we go again. Puppies must be taught, by their *mother,* their *littermates* and their *owner,* to inhibit biting while they still have those tiny, sharp puppy teeth. The routine goes like this: play—bite—reaction ("Ouch!" or scream, scowl), substitute a dog toy and ignore. Biting always ends with attention denied. A second offense gets the same treatment followed by a few minutes of ignoring. A puppy must *never* be allowed to get away with a hard bite; *that pup* must learn to control the bite. This is one ABC every puppy must learn—Acceptable Biting Control.

Another way to correct biting in a puppy is to pin the pup to the ground by placing one hand across the dog's shoulder and neck firmly enough to keep the dog grounded. The idea is to physically force the pup into submission. It's fine if you have a relatively small puppy or if you are six feet tall with the physique of a fullback and are capable of pinning a large, uncooperative dog. But if you can't do it successfully, the dog wins once again and you've lost another round. Don't even think of it with an aggressive dog! Because this is not the easiest method for the majority of dog owners, I've stuck with other less physical techniques that also work.

Question: "My dog is six years old and has never destroyed anything—until the other day. She chewed the toe of a brand-new pair of shoes I had just brought home from the store! I had put them on the floor in the kitchen because I was going to break them in while making dinner. What got into her?"

Answer: Your shoes were new, did not yet carry your scent and *they were on the floor.* The dog must have thought it was some new toy and *obviously* meant as a present for her. I'll bet she was nonplussed to be scolded!

Prevention: Think things through from the dog's viewpoint, so you won't end up blaming the dog for your own mistake. This is a bit of Prevention that holds true for just about everything else!

Question: "Doggone, a sort-of German Shepherd, has a very strange habit. Whenever he doesn't eat his entire meal, he begins what we call the mouth fetish, but this is really pushing the dish around with his nose, not his mouth. When playing with toys, he uses his mouth or paws, but to move the food dish, he just uses his nose. My husband says he's psychotic."

Answer: Don't call for a straightjacket yet. Your dog is just burying the leftovers. Canine species in the wild will eat as much as they can of the kill and bury the rest for later. The hole is dug using their feet, leftovers are dropped in and the cache covered up using their noses. Cats use their paws for both. To each his own.

Question: "Our mixed-breed dog has bitten two people and is considered to be vicious by anyone coming to the house, although he's usually okay with the family. We have a veterinarian who comes to the house, but even she suggested we keep the dog muzzled or have all his teeth removed. What are your thoughts on these two solutions?"

Answer: I am against removing a dog's teeth as a way to solve biting. It does nothing to remedy the real problem, which is aggression. You can use a strong basket-type muzzle for starters, but unless the dog can be retrained to eliminate all signs of aggression, you will never be able to relax your guard over such an animal.

Prevention: You can *prevent* aggressive behavior in an otherwise sound dog by firm, fair, nonaggressive (positive) teaching methods, but viciousness (harmful attacks without provocation) is not something for a pet owner to handle. A vicious dog is nothing more than a time bomb with a short fuse. Seek professional evaluation and face the fact that the only solution may be euthanasia.

Question: "Our dog bit a child who was teasing him by making the dog jump up for a toy, which she held out of reach. We kept telling her not to, but the dog bit her on the arm. The girl's family is furious and threatening to sue. What could we have done?"

Answer: You were right in trying to get the child to stop teasing. You could have separated the two with a Time-out, but that's hindsight. These things usually happen very quickly. Explain to the girl, her parents and your lawyer that the dog was *not* attacking her, but was only trying to get the toy the child was using to tease the dog.

Prevention: *Parents must teach their kids how to interact with animals,* instead of screaming "I'll sue!" when the kids get their comeuppance. A bit of Obedience training (for the girl) in this case might have helped, too.

8

SEPARATION ANXIETY

A modern phenomenon affecting our dogs is the proliferation of the working family. Mom and Dad put in a ten-hour workday, the kids have after-school jobs or activities, and during that entire long day nobody is home but the dog. These "latchkey pets" suffer from the same two things that affect the younger latchkey kids, namely, boredom and loneliness, but without access to video games, phone calls *or* a bathroom!

On top of all that is the dog's most common ailment called separation anxiety. It leaves the dog owner riddled with feelings of guilt and frustration. You can't make a phone call to Star to check on how she's doing, leave notes on the fridge or even explain a future concept such as you'll be back at six-thirty if the bus is on time. And ol' Star doesn't fare much better.

Boredom often occurs in conjunction with loneliness. It's the old "I've got nothing to do" situation, which translates into having nothing *interesting* to do, or having no one to do anything with. Loneliness is an emotional need with which some dogs can cope and others can't.

If you go down to the end of the town,
You must *never* go down without me.

—A. A. Milne, *When We Were Very Young*

Getting a second pet is no guarantee of a solution either (see Chapter 4). Two dogs left to their own devices can get into a heap of mischief. If separation anxiety is what causes your dog to destroy the house, bark all day—or just make you late for work—cure that *before* adding a playmate.

But take heart! Boredom and loneliness can be alleviated fairly easily. One of the most effective ways is to leave a radio on low volume and, don't laugh, preferably on a classical or "light" music station. My theory (totally empirical) is that the classical instruments emit natural sounds, whereas rock and rap rely on a heavy beat plus volume. Soft music and an occasional voice soothes dogs as well as dental patients! The lonely dog may wander around aimlessly for a short time and then, stoically perhaps, settle down to sleep. The bored dog will exhaust an entire supply of toys, perhaps slightly remodel a chair leg and also finally sleep. This is aimless, bored chewing, not to be confused with what's described next.

The dog suffering from the real stress of separation anxiety is driven to serious excesses. Unable to control the stress, the dog relieves it in any way possible—by excessive barking, house soiling or, in a fit of frustration, the total destruction of property: carpets and furniture chewed or ripped apart, walls gouged, curtains pulled down and shredded, and kitchen cabinets turned into firewood. This is *aggressive* behavior, whereas the other two (boredom and loneliness) are *passive*. There are various solutions for easing the stress of separation anxiety, but better yet, there are ways to prevent it.

Separation anxiety begins when an insecure Rufus first senses he is about to be left, and it builds up as the owner makes all those unconscious final preparations—checking lipstick or adjusting the tie, reaching for the car keys, a coat, a lunchbox, a briefcase, etc.—and moves toward the door. It can be precipitated by any separation and can last anywhere from a few minutes to hours after the owner has left. The destruction generally takes place soon after the owner leaves, with barking, whining and urinating (interspersed by an occasional nap) filling in the balance of the stressful hours.

The cure is primarily a matter of weaning the dog from overblown concern with your departure. The first thing to do is to minimize that event and change the rituals you go through so the dog's anxiety doesn't escalate as you proceed from alarm to shower to breakfast to closing the door behind you. Eliminate *all* forms of goodbyes, especially the long one that stems from your own guilt. A smiling "See you!" is a good note on which to leave any dog.

SATURATION

The Saturation process gets a section of its own here because it can be used to correct several other behavioral problems, not just separation anxiety. This method of behavior modification is also called flooding, or *desensitization.* I prefer Saturation only because that is exactly what you'll be doing—saturating the dog with so much of what it fears or hates that no more can be absorbed and the dog begins to relax and in the end to accept whatever form "the monster under the bed" may take.

Confine the dog to one room that is relatively dogproof, or at least one containing no irreplaceable possessions, and if possible, *not* the room from which you normally leave. A stressed-out dog cannot have the run of the house just yet and maybe never, because a whole houseful of emptiness triggers more stress! Dogs are "den" animals. Freedom is not what it's cracked up to be. *We* may like the idea of it, but to a dog it often means "freedom to get into trouble" and be punished or "freedom to become stressed out."

The entire scene that is the cause of anxiety (coming and going) must be toned down. Set aside a long weekend, or a vacation week. All members of the household should participate. For an hour at a time (or two if you can stand it), everyone leaves after making some of the normal everyday leave-taking preparations. One at a time each one returns at one-minute intervals as if you had forgotten something. You can chat among yourselves, but not to the dog. Do not look at the dog. No fond farewells; no gooey greetings. Limit goodbyes to one word: "Bye" or "See-ya" or "Ciao." On each return, greet the dog only casually if at all.

When Rufus begins to pay little or no attention to these comings and goings, you can very, *very* slowly work up to leaving him for ten minutes. Vary the length of time each person remains home and stays away. Your goal is to be able to leave the dog for over an hour without any signs of stress. After that goal is reached, the dog should be able to tolerate several hours alone and free of anxiety.

The saturation process can go on for hours over several days. When Rufus doesn't even glance up as you come or go, or grab your lunchbox, you'll know it's *beginning* to work. *Don't stop!* Keep it up for another couple of exits and entrances, and go at it again the next day, and the next, only letting up when you have reached your goal. Admittedly, this is a tedious process and it takes patience. Don't be upset when you need to backtrack now and then. You will! Return to a previous comfort level. This method is positive reinforcement, and *no* form of punishment is ever used.

You may have unintentionally built up anxiety in the dog by your own frantic rush to get to work on time, so this training may help to dispel "morning madness" for all members of the household. If it does, be sure to thank Rufus.

I said it is relatively easy to prevent, and it is if you play by the rules. Start on day one, the day your puppy or new older dog arrives in your home. Leave Ruffles confined to one area (preferably crated at first) while you and everyone in the household goes in and out of that area and in and out of the house without fanfare and for varying amounts of time. An occasional hello, but no goodbyes. *No* hello, and *no* release if there's whining or barking. *No* "freedom," except in a safe, confined area. But there's good news. A puppy trained to accept your comings and goings can get an enthusiastic greeting to celebrate your return.

There are other causes of separation anxiety, which are covered in the Questions and Answers in this chapter.

PARTING COMPANY

Question: "I've been late for work more times than I care to admit because my dog, Visa (his father was Amex), gets so upset at my leaving. He cries and whines and looks so forelorn that I sometimes spend as much as half an hour trying to console him. This is getting serious! What can I do before I get fired?"

Answer: All your words of comfort, all the guilt, all that sweet-talk—saying you'll be right back, that you know how lonely it will be, that you wish you could take the dog to work, that you'll miss him, too—only prolongs the agony and causes the tension and stress to build.

Prevention: "Goodbye" is one word. Use it.

Question: "Our dog is twelve years old, a female mixed-breed. Our neighbors tell us she has started whining, crying and howling as soon as we leave in the morning. She never did this before. We have always lived in the same house, and we all work about the same hours. Why is she doing this and what can we do about it?"

Answer: A nonscientific answer might be the age factor, that when dogs get on in years, begin to lose hearing, sight and agility, perhaps sensing their own vulnerability, they want the reassuring presence of their family or "pack." Or there may be no known cause.

Change the dog's routine. Give her a short brisk walk in the morning, and if you normally only feed in the evening, divide the amount in half so you can leave her

"Don't leave me! Come back! Please?"

with breakfast. Leave a radio on. That may be change enough. Or hire a pet-sitter to give the dog a midday break. And you need to face the fact that possibly nothing at all will help.

Prevention: There is no Prevention because there's no way to stop the clock. The best you can do is to see it coming, maintain the dog's physical health and mental outlook through play, walks, etc., and accept the normal, often unexplainable changes that will take place in a dog's later years.

Question: "My 105-pound, three-year-old Labrador-mix steals food off the table, jumps on people (for joy), but bites and claws at me when I leave for work. We've been to Obedience school and worked with a trainer. In both situations he's an angel. The jumping on others is getting better because I put him in his crate when guests arrive. But I do have to go to work!"

Answer: Your dog is pushing your buttons. When it's just the two of you, that Angel turns into Authority. Biting is an emphatic canine method of disciplining *you*. Crating the dog may solve *your* problem, but it's not teaching the dog the acceptable way to greet people. Work with your trainer (and the Saturation process) to stop the jumping up and separation anxiety problems.

Stealing food requires entrapment (see Chapter 2).

Prevention: Teach! Never punish or correct without an immediate lesson in what you *want* the dog to do. A dog must be taught to greet people by sitting or standing quietly. The day you get a dog it must be taught that saying hello nicely earns pats and praise, that you will come and go, that stealing is a crime and the first-time culprit gets a lesson in How To Behave. The next mistake gets a Time-out. Teach a special signal if you like your dog to jump up on you. My dogs are medium-size, and I enjoy a rousing greeting, so I use "High five!" as a signal to let them know it's okay to give me a wild and crazy kind of welcome.

Question: "We bought a Toy Poodle puppy from a breeder with several children. He's adorable, but he's driving us nuts. We leave him in the basement while at work and also at night. He screams most of the time! His area in the basement is about 20' × 6', which should be big enough for a three-pound pup. There's a dog bed at one end. What do you suppose is wrong with him?"

Answer: Look at it from the pup's point of view. Until you bought him, he was with other dogs and people, safely confined, but where he could see and hear all the activity of the house. Now he is in solitary confinement for most of every twenty-four hours. No wonder he screams! Let the pup sleep in a *small* crate in your bedroom. Don't talk to him at all after he's been put to bed. If there's any fussing, tap on the crate and say "No!" firmly. Nothing more. Knowing you are nearby, he will settle down by the time you've put out the light, if not the first night, then soon.

A radio in the basement will ease the puppy's daytime isolation. I assume, given your present routine, that you are housetraining the puppy using newspapers, and with that problem solved, you might consider getting a second puppy to provide the company your pup needs.

Prevention: Dogs, particularly puppies, are social animals. It is unnatural and frightening for a puppy to be left alone all day and all night. A noontime walk and playtime would break up the day, and the proximity of family members at night allows the dog to be part of the family and to relax.

Question: "We purchased an eleven-week-old Shih Tzu puppy. She was easily housetrained, learned all her Obedience commands quickly, as well as a lot of fun things, and also caught on to our work routine. Now she is eleven months old and suddenly does not want us to leave in the morning. It breaks my heart to see her so sad. I hate to go. We thought about getting another dog, but they might not get along, and frankly, I'm not up to it. What can we do?"

Answer: Congratulations! You're doing a great job of training and enjoying the puppy and now you have reached the "teenager" phase. Treat it casually and cheerfully. Don't fall for the sad look, or for any other uncooperative little trick this clever pup dreams up. As an act of kindness, since both are forms of communication, keep your hands and eyes off the dog for five minutes or so before you leave. A happy one-word farewell and out you go.

Prevention: The biggest mistake is to fall for one more goodbye. Don't do it! Keep it short and simple. "Ciao, baby."

Question: "When we leave for work, I make sure the dog has plenty of toys to occupy her while we're gone. She must have twenty-five or thirty toys spread all over the house, but it doesn't help. My neighbor tells me she barks, and she has destroyed the back door and the windowsills. Why doesn't she play when we are out?"

Answer: See all the previous Answers for suggestions on relieving separation anxiety and confinement, and add one more. Instead of leaving her with a houseful (or a roomful) of toys, limit her to three or four and then change them every few days. Variety, not quantity, is the spice of a dog's life.

TRAVEL

There are other forms of separation that can cause anxiety. Roxanne will be a happy camper when she learns to travel in the car quietly, and to stay in a boarding kennel or veterinary hospital without undue stress.

QUESTIONS, SUGGESTIONS, SOLUTIONS

Question: "About a year ago I gave up taking my dog any-where in the car. She barks, jumps all over the seats, pants, drools, and as if all that weren't bad enough, if I leave her for two minutes, she digs holes in the seats. I think she's psychotic, but is there a cure?"

Answer: She's not, and yes there certainly is. Start by putting the dog in a seat belt, or harness on the front seat. Get in on your side and read a magazine. Turn on the radio. Sit quietly, paying no attention to the dog. When she is quiet, end the session with a short walk and playtime.

Repeat several times for a couple of days before starting the engine. Don't go anywhere. When the dog can accept that, turn the motor off, get out of the car by yourself and walk around the car a few times (inspect the tires or some such). End the session with a walk for you *and* your dog as before.

When all of that can be done in peace and quiet, ease out of your driveway and park in front of the house. End as before. After several such trips, go a bit further down the street. Be very observant and quit at the first sign of stress, ending with a walk or play. The dog's behavior is correct when she (finally!) thinks car trips are fun. *No* punishments, verbal or otherwise. *No* petting. Cheerful chitchat comes later.

Prevention: You get the idea. It's Saturation! Don't be upset when the dog quits. The method doesn't take you along 1-2-3-4-5. It's more like 1-2-1-2-3-2-2-3, etc. Proceed at the dog's comfort level. It's hard for Roxanne to learn not to be afraid!

Question: "We're going away for the holidays and our Airedale has never stayed in a boarding kennel before. Are there any tips for making it a pleasant experience for her?"

Answer: Call the boarding kennel and arrange to see it. Ask questions such as: Where do the dogs sleep? (Usually in crates, or beds in stalls.) Will your dog be kept on the same food you feed? What veterinarian is on call or will they contact yours? What is the daily routine? This last question is important, so write it down and make note of how it differs from your own, primarily wake-up time, dinnertime and bedtime (three essential parts of a dog's day). Are they members of ABKA (the American Boarding Kennel Association)? Do they offer grooming? Your dog might enjoy this personal attention.

Don't even consider a boarding kennel that you feel "iffy" about. Like what you see and hear, or go elsewhere. Then get the dog ready for the separation. If dogs are crated, get out the crate and reintroduce the regimen of being crated at night. With a good-night, "Good dog" biscuit, of course. Begin to adjust the dog's schedule to that of the boarding kennel.

Take along something in the way of a security blanket—an old toy, a used (not freshly laundered) towel or other bedding. You may not get the item back, so don't leave anything of value. Hand the dog's leash over to the kennel person with a cheery "Good girl!"

Prevention: All of the above will help to prevent separation anxiety. One other tip: Drop your pet off in the early morning so the dog has all day to get used to the staff and the smells, sights and sounds of the new surroundings.

Question: "I'm flying from New York to Florida and will be taking my Maltese with me. The airline gave me their rules, but what should I know for the dog's sake? She's my spoiled baby."

Answer: Lucky you! Tiny dogs can go into carriers that fit under the seat for take-off, landing and during meals, instead of going into the cargo bay. Let her get used to the carrier gradually until she will stay quietly for an hour or so. Do *not* feed her prior to your flight.

Prevention: There is none, other than cautions for owners of larger dogs.

- Move mountains to get nonstop flights.
- Let all airline personnel know that *you* know live animals are last loaded and first off.
- Dogs are never, ever to be left on the tarmac.
- They should not be put on the baggage carousel, but hand-carried or brought in on a cart.

Question: "My wife and I are renting a small motor home and will travel across country for six weeks, taking our Cardigan Welsh Corgi with us. All three of us are new to this kind of travel, so we don't even know what questions to ask. Can you help?"

Answer: Pack for the dog:
1. Dog bowls
2. Food for at least a week
3. Bottled water (dogs get tummy upsets, too)

4. A couple of big dog towels for rainy days or when swimming is on the agenda
5. The dog's immunizations, including rabies, should be
   updated
6. Rabies tag, dog license and ID kept on the dog's collar

In case you suddenly want to cross into Canada or
Mexico, get a health certificate from your vet, and keep
it along with a clear photo of the dog in the glove
compartment.

Take along an extra collar and leash and check the con-
dition of the one being worn. Away from home every dog
needs the safety of a leash. A crate is a boon on such a
trip. Wherever you stop and can't take the dog (rest stops,
dinner, museums, etc.) leave the dog crated, park in the
shade and leave windows open. (Remember, your motor
home is a rental!) Enjoy!

Prevention: Crate-trained dogs can go everywhere happily and safely.

OTHER SEPARATIONS

The dog caught in the middle of a divorce is subject to a lot of
stress, not only that of separation, but because the people
involved in a divorce are generally so caught up in their own
personal conflict, they may not be sensitive to the needs of
ol' Rufus.

Question: "I was just divorced, and my ex-husband took the
dog because he says he paid for it. However, Mitsy was
bought as a present for the children, and they are heartbroken. They won't even discuss getting another dog.

They want Mitsy. To be honest, I never even thought about it until it was too late."

Answer: It would have been better had the dog been left with the kids (I strongly advocate this if at all possible), but the barn door has closed. Wait it out and when the time is right, involve the children in selecting a dog. They're older now than when Mitsy arrived, so they might decide on a totally different breed. Your library has many books to browse through like the American Kennel Club *Complete Dog Book,* but local dog shows are where you'll see lots of breeds and be able to talk to breeders.

Prevention: Dogs, *especially* any dog that is *a child's pet,* should be carefully considered before being included in a divorce settlement as an afterthought. When their adult parents are proving not to be superhuman beings after all, and the world is falling apart, kids need their confidante and faithful companion more than ever. This is not the time to haggle. If your offspring are attached to Rufus, he's their dog and will be the best therapy to get them over the family's breakup.

Question: "My husband bought me a puppy when we were engaged. We were married for three years and are now divorced. I was the major caretaker, but the dog is going through some kind of anxiety crisis! About an hour before the normal time my 'ex' used to come home, the dog begins watching for him. Then he whines and paces and I can't distract him with toys or food. He has always been *my* dog, but now I wonder! What should I do?"

Answer: All dogs are from Missouri. *Show,* don't tell him. Show the dog that life alone with you will be great. Go for fun walks in new areas—park, beach, woods or country road. (City streets are pretty much all alike, but if that's where you are, try some new ones.) Take the dog back to school: Obedience, Agility, Tracking, whatever you're up to. Of course, there's also therapy for *you* in all of this.

Prevention: Whenever possible, wean the dog from some of the things that have changed. Then the dog can get used to a few new routines at a time, while the rest of life stays in place. The most important thing to a dog is the consistent routine of the human pack leaders.

Question: "Friends of mine were divorced and I adopted their dog, whom I've known for six years. The only problem is her whining. She gets started and works herself up into a unconsolable frenzy! I checked with my friends and the dog had never behaved this way before. What can I do?"

Answer: This is a common behavioral problem in any adopted dog, whether the dog is a best friend or total stranger. The dog is saying, "It's been nice visiting with you, but now please take me home." You can't, but you can provide distractions (silly *and* serious play activities) and additional exercise, and, if warranted, consult your vet about giving the dog a very mild tranquilizer just to get her through the transitional period.

Remain cheerful and matter of fact. Again, don't say the kind of thing you'd say to a child, like "Poor Penny, would my poor sad baby like a cookie or maybe a walk?" She's miserable enough, so instead go overboard in the other direction. Be upbeat: "Hey Penny! Time for a walk. Let's go!"

Prevention: There is no guaranteed way to prevent homesickness. The majority of dogs walk into their new home, do a detailed inspection, find the most comfortable spot to claim as their own and settle in for life. No doubt that's pretty much how it all began when dogs first accepted us as their companions.

9

BREED SPECIFICS

This will be a very short section, because as soon as I make a statement about *anything* being "breed specific," ninety-nine examples will surface to disprove it! The truth of the matter is that *dogs are dogs,* and while different breeds of dogs have been bred (some for centuries) to do specific jobs, not every individual within any one breed has had those talents developed. Even those that have utilized their innate abilities will vary greatly in their skills. So we have Herding dogs that can't herd anything, Terriers that cry "Eeek!" at mice, gun dogs that are shy of cap guns, Toy breeds that don't care to be toyed with and Hounds that wouldn't hound a flea.

Some dogs will make an attempt to be all things on all occasions. Two examples of this are under my desk: a male Welsh Terrier who regularly points pheasant, and, less surprisingly, a second Welsh who hunts birds like a cat—prowl and pounce. Both dogs herd kids, and—so as not to be a total embarrassment to their breed—both also go to ground after rabbit and woodchuck.

This above all: to thine own self be true;
And it must follow, as the night the day,
Thou canst not then be false to any man.

—William Shakespeare, *Hamlet*

As in cases of mistaken identity, behaviors that *are* typical of a breed are often the only complaint the owner has with a dog. Conversely, atypical behavior may be a dog's most endearing quality. The most flat-footed statement that can be made about breed specifics is that by selecting a certain breed as a pet, you limit the range of variations attributable to inheritance. The balance are dictated by environment and early exposure to learning. Fortunately, all that most people want in a dog is a well-behaved pet plus what they consider good looks.

While a dog's general behavior normally reflects its breed, honing breed-specific skills requires much training (of the owner, too) plus the opportunity to put it all to use. In order to understand why your dog, Drummer, does or doesn't do certain things, you need to accept the fact that Drummer is a dog first, and a Labrador Retriever second. Then, of course, he may be a dog first, a *pet* second and a Lab third, depending on where you have placed the emphasis in teaching anything beyond housetraining.

It goes without saying that a Retriever will be calmer than a Terrier, a Toy dog more vocal than a giant, but these basic characteristics may not be given a minute's consideration by the average pet buyer. Looks are what count. Prospective pet buyers are apt to fall for the gorgeous coat, soulful eyes or funny facial expression (or sad or serious or intelligent or whatever). They may not even know the name of the breed or have any other knowledge of the characteristics, or care. Add to this the plight of the mixed-breed dog whose looks may indicate one thing, but whose unseen genes are saying something else. Is it any wonder pet owners come up against behavioral problems!

Working breeds are generally happiest when given a job. This Giant Schnauzer could find employment almost anywhere.

DOIN' WHAT COMES NATURALLY?

Question: "My sweet-tempered Samoyed is kept outside, but he digs big holes even when the ground is muddy. He stops when I say to, but as soon as I leave he's at it again. How can I control this?"

Answer: Northern breeds, of which the Samoyed is one, are apt to be diggers. The "specific" here is the dog's need to make a sleeping nest in a snowbank in order to be warm and protected, but a pure white dog that's been digging in a muddy pen can't make a very desirable companion! The only way to break the habit is to bring the dog indoors (a cool basement or garage will do) and correct every attempt to dig outdoors. A better alternative is to resurface the floor of the dog run. Or buy a sled!

Prevention: Dealing with a breed-specific digger is easier to prepare for than to correct. Attach a dog run alongside the house or garage, with a dog door allowing access to an inside area (as small as a dog house or as large as you wish). Lay turkey wire on the ground of the run and top it with twelve to eighteen inches of crushed stone, or pour a cement base. It's dig proof and easy to keep clean, and the dog won't get muddy.

Question: "I have a German Shepherd puppy (seven months). She is obedient and very gentle, but no watchdog. She never barks. I don't want her to be ferocious, but when someone is at the door, she responds with a wagging tail and greets strangers like long-lost friends. What am I doing wrong?"

Answer: Be thankful she is friendly and outgoing at this age. When your puppy grows up, some of her watchdog capabilities will kick in naturally.

Prevention: Do *not* teach a young puppy to bark unless you want to spend the next ten years trying to make it stop!

Question: "I have a six-year-old Sheltie (Shetland Sheepdog). He has done advanced Obedience work (Open), but I cannot stop him from herding guests when they stand up to leave. He sometimes gives a little nip at their pants leg as if to get them moving. I'm afraid one day someone will get bitten, so now I put the dog outside just before guests are ready to go."

Answer: Many dogs in the Herding breeds do this when given the chance. It is in the genes and completely normal. They do it to children at play, and people moving anywhere on the dogs' turf. Your dog is well trained, so put him on a Down-Stay before your guests prepare to leave.

Prevention: Teaching social skills sometimes includes going against the breed-specific ones. Putting the dog outside is a cop-out, an easy way to get out of teaching what's wanted.

Question: "Our beautiful yellow Labrador Retriever will not retrieve any single thing we have ever tossed for him outdoors. He will sometimes retrieve (or catch is more like it) bits of food in the house but is soon bored. We have tried teaching him to swim, but he hates the water! He's good in Obedience and loves agility, except for anything that is high off the ground. We are getting a chocolate Lab female (from stock bred for hunting) and hope she'll teach him. We sure can't!"

Answer: Enjoy your dog for what he is—a beautiful, easygoing, laid-back Lab. The new puppy may (MAY) fulfill your other dreams. A companion MAY inspire participation in retrieving and swimming, but don't hold your

A Labrador puppy fitted with a harness for an introduction to Tracking in fields.

breath. Ol' Yellow will have a few ideas of his own as to what Li'l Semisweet needs to be taught.

Prevention: Dogs within any breed are individuals. Some more so than others. There is no perfect rose.

Question: "I'd like to have my two-year-old Chow Chow neutered, but I'm afraid it might adversely affect his temperament. He is aloof with strangers and walks away from small children, but if they come too close, he will growl. I don't want any child to be bitten."

Answer: Neutering is only one hundred percent effective in eliminating the dog's ability to reproduce. Everything else is qualitative, not by breed, but on an individual basis. All kinds of claims are made as to changes that occur in dogs after neutering, most attributable to the owners' aspirations, not to the surgical procedure. Some say the dog is more easygoing, others that the dog stops marking territory (thus no longer lifts its leg in the house). Others swear there is little or no difference. However, I have never heard of this minor operation causing a dog to become more aggressive. I'd say you have everything to gain and *nothing to lose.*

Prevention: More and more breeders and veterinarians advocate early spay/neutering. It used to be six to seven months of age; now five to six months is the norm and as early as eight weeks in some cases. The obvious "prevention" is that of unwanted puppies, with a side benefit of "neutralizing" the temperament. But the big bonus is the virtual elimination of ovarian or testicular cancer.

Question: "We have a Collie. He does very well in Obedience and when I'm training him at home. The problem is when the whole family goes for a walk. He constantly wants to walk in back of us or off to the side. Are we wrong in expecting him to maintain a Heel position?"

Answer: Family walks are for fun, fresh air and exercise, not Obedience training. Your dog is doing what comes naturally—herding your family. Let him do the job as he sees it. Dogs may have been the founders of the "job satisfaction" theory.

Prevention: Walks should be at least ninety-five percent pure pleasure for the dog—stopping, sniffing, investigating—and for some breeds this may include a job assignment in connection with some form of training. Using a Flexi-Leash (retractable) tells a dog he's out for a sniff-and-enjoy kind of jaunt.

Question: "My Obedience-trained Pomeranian was calm until he was neutered. Now he jumps up on people, barks nonstop, even growls. When I pick him up, he's quiet. What happened to my nice quiet dog?"

Answer: These changes have little or nothing to do with neutering and more to do with your own reactions to the unwanted behavior. *Do not pick up a stressed-out small dog!* (I wish I could get that warning across to all small dog owners.) It gives the dog many wrong signals. For example, that *you* are afraid, or that *you* approve of the way the dog is carrying on and *you* want to protect *him.* It elevates the dog to your height, giving the dog a grossly enlarged idea of its own size and importance. As if that's not enough, you put yourself in real danger of being bitten in the face.

Prevention: Using Obedience commands, keep the dog four-on-the-floor, on leash (see Chapter 8 for Saturation and Chapter 3 for Aggression).

Question: "Whenever my German Shorthaired Pointer gets near a squirrel or bird, she goes off into her own world. She won't listen to me at all, which recently almost cost her her life. Is there any way to curb her instinctual behavior?"

Answer: It's possible, but your success depends upon how hard you want to work on it. Contact a trainer who specializes in hunting dogs to teach you how to call the dog off prey.

Prevention: Know *ALL* about a breed before venturing into ownership and watch for the first signs of any behaviors you want to modify. You can't "prevent" Mother Nature from doing her thing, but you can alter most behaviors to levels that are acceptable to you.

Question: "I adore my beautiful blue-eyed Siberian Husky, but she drives me crazy with her whining. Also, I can't keep her in the house because she chews everything. But outdoors she digs her way out. If I try to walk her, she pulls me like a sled down the street. She flunked Obedience. And she won't eat! I don't know where to begin."

Answer: You could begin by recognizing that all the things you mention are typical, breed-specific components of a Siberian Husky. These are generally outdoor dogs, so keep her outside (but check on her from time to time and check your fences daily) and bring her indoors when you are free to supervise her in-house manners. Use a head collar such as the Halti to ease her sled-pulling zeal (or buy a sled and hitch a ride). Save your money and frustration—Siberians have small appetites. Lastly, get as much as you can out of Obedience and forget perfection!

Prevention: Feel better?

Question: "I bought a Rottweiler because I was told they need a lot of exercise. The dog is now almost five months old and he can't even keep up with me when I'm jogging. He hides under the bed when I'm getting ready, so obviously he doesn't even like exercise!"

Answer: Not only did you get the wrong breed, you are asking a pup to do a dog's work. Rotties are strong, muscular dogs but not natural runners. Look to the Northern breeds, or Dalmatians or some of the slightly built hunting dogs.

Prevention: No puppy of any breed should be jogging at such a young age. Dogs do not fully mature until they are two to three years of age. Gentle training can begin at about ten months to a year but *only* after a complete physical exam, including a veterinarian's check of shoulders, hips, elbows and stifles for soundness.

Question: "Our female Golden Retriever left many patches of dead grass where she urinated on the lawn. We have since sold her (for other reasons) and plan to get a male Standard Poodle. I've heard that their habit of marking is bad for shrubs and trees, but what about the lawn?"

Answer: To say the least, this is an unusual way to buy a dog! Any breed of dog, and either sex (spayed or neutered), produces urine that will kill small vegetation and burn larger varieties. On the other hand, a cat digs small neat holes in the flower beds and buries its excrement. Perhaps that would suit you better. A statue of any breed would look nice and not damage the lawn.

Prevention: Set aside an area of crushed stone (attractively fenced and bordered with flowers) and take the pup there on leash when housetraining. You have to be there to say "Good dog" *as* the dog eliminates. But all dogs (male and female) of every breed will mark

territory with drops of urine, and it would be very difficult to train a dog *never* to eliminate on its own property.

Question: "How can I teach my Soft Coated Wheaten Terrier
not to jump up? It was okay when she was a puppy, but
she's two years old and still doing it."

Answer: This is so much a part of the breed that it has
been given a name: the Wheaten Welcome. It's a lot easier
to accept than to eliminate! Using Off and Sit with treat
rewards may help if you are an exceptionally good trainer.
Or take one front paw in each hand and hold them very
firmly (just short of squeezing) while you smile and say
hello in a cheerful voice. Most dogs will try to get away,
so *as* you release the paws, still smiling, say, "OFF!
GOOOOD off!"

Prevention: It would seem a pity to eradicate such a
charismatic characteristic of the breed. Accept the
Wheaten Welcome as part and parcel of the breed you
bought.

*Peebles, a Border Terrier doing what comes naturally—Chasing a lure,
even through bales of hay.*

Question: "Our West Highland White Terrier almost caught a mouse as it disappeared under a closet door. That was a year ago. He still sits outside that closet with his nose glued to the space beneath the door. How can I convince him to give it up?"

Answer: Once a terrier has seen or heard a mouse or other vermin, it will continue to keep watch at that place almost forever after. How else is a Terrier going to catch a mouse? Tenacity is the Terrier's other name.

Prevention: All puppies should be taught the life-saving commands, one of which is "Leave it!," which can also be used in an attempt to break a dedicated mouse watcher.

Question: "I know a Golden Retriever is meant to retrieve, but I thought only things like dead birds! We taught ours to bring in the newspaper and now she is bringing home the contents of our neighbors' garages. How do we stop our overachiever Retriever?"

Answer: You've got the wrong label. It's not retrieving. It's called stealing. The first is breed specific; the second is a punishable offense. The solution is easy. It's called a leash. Retrieving your newspaper is rewarded by those two little words, "Thank you." All other exercise for your retrieving zealot must be limited to your own backyard, unless you are into brisk walks long enough to give the dog a workout.

Prevention: Excuses, excuses! The first time your Golden Gadabout arrived home with anything other than the newspaper, I'll bet you all roared with laughter. She should have been firmly disciplined with a scowling "Leave it!" And not let out alone. (*Then* you could all roar with laughter.)

10

CHILDREN'S CORNER

Children and dogs should go together like peanut butter and jelly, but sometimes either combination can get sticky. In order to avoid a calamity, there are three basic rules:

1. Children must be taught how to treat dogs (their own and others).
2. The responsibility given to a child for a pet's care must not exceed the child's own maturity and capability.
3. Parents must be prepared to step in quickly, quietly and without reprimand when (2) falls apart.

Even a very nice youngster of four or five can occasionally be spiteful, dictatorial and mean. With only the dog lower on the social scale than little Marie, she will vent her fury on poor Rufus. Too often this unfair attack on Rufus is compounded when Mom lays into the dog for growling but says nothing to ornery little Marie!

It's not difficult to teach youngsters to be responsible pet owners, but it takes time, some knowledge on the part of the

"Every dog has his day."
[Preferably with a child!]

parents and a whole heap of patience. Be realistic. No five-year-old, no matter how angelic, brilliant, loving, capable, etc., can fully take care of a dog.

All small kids, however, should be taught how to approach someone else's dog (only with permission and an adult present), how to pet a dog (very gently with a hand, not hugs and kisses) and how to help brush, feed and water their own dog. **Dogs are not toys,** and small dogs cannot be endlessly carried about—or thoughtlessly dropped! Not all large dogs appreciate kids climbing over them or trying to ride bareback. It is safer to assume that dogs, particularly strange ones (and even Grandpa's or Aunt Minnie's), do not feel comfortable having their space invaded.

Older children of eight, nine or ten who are inundated with afterschool activities cannot be expected to take on the full-time responsibility of a pet, and problems will arise if parents expect it. The charm of a child's life (at least as adults look back on it) is in large part its carefree flexibility. A child's dog is a pal, a coconspirator, a confidante and an understanding, totally uncritical peer. In turn, the child—with good adult examples—learns to be considerate, nurturing, trustworthy, sharing, understanding and less critical.

COMING OF AGE

If one age is "more perfect" than any other, it is probably the range from seven to ten. The desire to own a dog has been growing. The child of ten is now physically and mentally capable of tackling some, even most, of the care and training of a pet. Not entirely; not twenty-four hours a day and not 365 days a year, although some seven-, eight- or nine-year-olds do very well if they are allowed occasional lapses without recrimination. Ten-year-olds do even better. Keep in mind it's a "family" dog.

Part of the parents' responsibility is praise for a job—if it's well done. Only give Kathy as much to do for Rufus as she can handle and offer sincere appreciation when it is warranted. Kids are just as savvy as dogs in knowing when you're faking it. False or profuse praise is actually worse than none at all.

Here are some of the things kids can do for and with their dogs:

- Prepare meals. Measure the food—great for math skills.
- Keep fresh, clean water available all day.
- Wash the water bowl and food pan.
- Brush and comb the dog at least once a week, checking for fleas, ticks and mats.
- Attend Obedience classes. (Those especially geared to kids or for the whole family are ideal.)
- Walk the dog (only where and when this is safe, for example, after the dog is trained and *never* alone in traffic).
- Learn more about the breed, or dogs in general, from library books—increases reading skills and enjoyment.
- Attend dog shows, Frisbee contests and agility competitions. And on, and on!

Many rules for good behavior in our children also apply to our dogs. For example:

- Say hello nicely. (Don't bark at our guests.)
- Be pleasant at the table. (Don't growl over your food.)
- Come when you're called. (Come when you're called.)
- Keep your feet off the furniture. (Keep off the furniture!)

The list of parallels is endless.

DOGS AND KIDS

Question: "My dog, Jiggers, won't come when he's called. My dad gets mad at me because Jiggers runs off. How can I teach him?"

Answer: Keep Jiggers *on leash* and make coming to you a fun game. Always call him with a big smile. Crouch down and open your arms wide as you say, "**Come!** *Good* dog!" In the house, whenever you see him coming toward you (perhaps when he hears you pick up his dinner dish), say, "Jiggers, come! Good dog." Remember to smile and sound happy whenever you call him.

Children develop a very special bond with their dogs.

Prevention: The biggest mistake *everyone* makes (Moms and Dads included) is to call the dog at the wrong time. Never—*never*—*N-E-V-E-R* call a dog to come *to* you for a punishment. And before the dog is completely reliable, never say "Come" if you can't enforce the command. Keeping the dog on leash gives you the necessary control. A dog will often test you to see what happens if she *doesn't* come. If this occurs with the dog off leash, you may become angry or end up playing canine catch-me-if-you-can, but no matter what, the dog wins and has only learned how to disobey you.

Question: "My dog runs away a lot even though we punish him when he finally comes home. Why doesn't he learn not to run away?"

Answer: He *has* learned exactly *what you've taught him*—that *he gets punished* for coming home. If he gets away again, don't use any form of punishment. Always show him how happy you are to see him. Mend your fences or walk your dog on leash.

Prevention: Fences and leashes are what keep dogs safe and at home.

Question: "My older brother hits Chaz when the dog does anything my brother doesn't like. Lately Chaz has started growling at him, so my brother just hits the dog more. What can I do about it? Chaz is a real neat dog."

Answer: It's time for Mom and Dad to lay down the law and teach your brother how to behave toward the dog. If not, the dog will certainly bite him, and *for good reason.* Perhaps you can find out about 4-H Obedience classes and establish a good working relationship yourself with Chaz, so you can keep the dog out of your brother's way until your "older" brother grows up.

Prevention: Never hit a dog for misbehaving. *Teach* what you want the dog to do. Hitting a dog for growling is stupid—and dangerous. The growl is a warning signal. A bite comes next.

Question: "We live near a park. Dogs are allowed in the park, but they have to be on leash. I'd like to let my dog run free. I'm twelve and my dog is very good. Why is there such a stupid law?"

Answer: It's a *sensible* law because it considers the safety of all the dogs and all the people. Some dogs might run off and get lost, others might fight and get hurt, or knock down small kids (or frail adults). Also, by keeping the dog on leash, everyone can pick up after his or her own dog, leaving the park clean for those unfortunate people who don't have dogs.

Prevention: Such laws *are* preventions. It is a shame that not all dogs are well socialized and trained, and that not all dog owners are as responsible as you are, but being a responsible dog owner also means obeying things like leash laws.

Question: "We have a gentle, obedient Rottweiler that the kids take to 4-H. We'd like to get a second dog, but my eleven-year-old daughter was bitten and badly frightened by a friend's dog not long ago, so we were thinking of a small puppy. Do you think our Rottie would be too big and strong for a puppy? And what do you think about a puppy with kids (four of them)?"

Answer: Go for it! Dogs that are good with children are likely to be good with puppies, especially because a puppy will naturally be submissive to the older resident dog.

Assuming you know what caused the attack by a friend's dog and have eliminated the possibility of it happening again, let your daughter be the pup's trainer in order to get rid of any fears she may still have. Talking it out helps, but she needs to prove to herself she really can do it.

Prevention: Being bitten by a dog is like being thrown from a horse—the sooner you return to working with the animal, the better. A puppy is the way to go. Just remind all the kids that puppies have needle-sharp teeth that can scratch as well as bite. Puppies must be taught the rules about biting (see Chapter 7).

Question: "My dog doesn't like me. I'm in school all day, so my Mom takes care of him. If I try to pick him up, or get him to play with me, he just growls. How can I make him like me?"

Answer: You *can't make* a dog like you. Obviously, he's a dog that doesn't care to be picked up, so do things with him on the floor or outdoors. Perhaps you are trying too hard, or forcing yourself on the dog. Put on a great big smile and a happy voice. (Dogs don't like grumps!) Start with something he already knows so you can *begin with praise—and a treat.* Gently show what you'd like him to do. Then begin to teach your dog some tricks such as hide-and-seek, tag (outdoors, please!), roll over, etc. Be generous with Good dog when he gets it right.

Prevention: Children need to be taught how to discipline (i.e., teach, not punish) their dog in order to have a well-defined, trusting relationship. If Bobby is not taught how to interact with Rufus, chances are the dog will become dominant or disobedient and Bobby will feel like he's a failure.

Question: "I am fourteen years old and have a six-year-old dog. The dog stays outside all day and night because my Mom didn't want a dog. I know he needs more than food and a bed, so I brush him and walk him, but I'd like to get into Obedience. Mom will now let me bring him in the house for an hour, but after ten minutes he wants to go out. I can only brush him or pet him for a few minutes, then he walks away. He won't play any games at all. I thought Bassets were affectionate. He's not. What's his problem?"

Answer: He can't change his attitude toward life all at once. He doesn't feel comfortable being indoors because he has always been outside. I'd guess that no one played with him regularly and taught him games when he was a young pup, eager to learn. Think of him now as sort of a canine illiterate in need of patient educating. Bassets are affectionate, but the dog/human bond is developed in a dog at the age of six to ten *weeks,* not years. Bassets are built to do a lot of sitting, and perhaps the problem has to do with the fact that as a teenager you have more get-up-and-go than a middle-aged Basset.

Prevention: Kids' dogs should not be isolated outdoors; they belong wherever the kids are, sharing in learning about being part of a family.

Question: "I have a two-year-old neutered male that I show at 4-H. He was doing all kinds of winning for two years. At the last show, he wouldn't even listen to me. When we got home, he was normal. I took him to a costume party and the same thing happened. What's making him act this way?"

Answer: Give him a rest. He's not bad, just bored. Could it be that *you* are not making it as much fun as you did at first?

Prevention: Working dogs need time off.

Question: "I have one dog and would like to learn more about caring for animals because I want to be a vet. Where can I start? I'm just fifteen."

Answer: You could begin by working after school and during vacations in a boarding kennel, grooming shop, Obedience school, shelter or possibly a veterinary hospital. The jobs you'll be offered won't be glamorous, but every one of these people now in charge most likely began the same way. Ask your own veterinarian for suggestions. Good luck!

Prevention: Whew! At last! A problem without a need for prevention!

Question: "Our dog is part Chihuahua, part Dachshund. Every time my brother and I play rough, the dog jumps up snarling and snapping. Is he being protective?"

Answer: No, it's more like he's refereeing what he sees as a fight. However, the dog could easily bite one of you because he doesn't know your rules. Put the dog in another room before you and your brother begin to roughhouse.

Prevention: Crates were made for just such events. Sometimes it's the referee who needs a Time-out.

Question: "I have two half-German half-Alaskan puppies and when I try to give them a bath, they holler and try to run away. Could you please send me directions?"

Answer: Brushing will get them almost as clean as bathing them and it will teach them to stand still and let you do it. Leave one pup in the house and put the other up off the ground on a bench or a low steady table, so you can reach the entire dog. All pups need gentle handling, but *gradually* work up to a thorough brushing and combing. This will clean the coat. You might want to use a flea spray (very carefully, with help from an adult) and then put your nice cleaned-up puppy in the house and go to work on the other one.

Prevention: Lots of dogs do not like to get wet. Dogs that must be professionally groomed on a regular basis should be introduced to the groomer at ten or twelve weeks of age, just to get used to the place, the person, being handled, etc.

Question: "We have an exceptionally well-behaved Bullmastiff (eighteen months old). The only problem is that every day when my young son comes home from school, the dog lowers his head and growls. Any other time they are inseparable playmates. How should we correct the dog?"

Answer: *Don't* correct the dog. Give your son a few treats to keep in his pocket so he can walk into the house with a treat on the open palm of his hand. In a bright cheery voice, he can greet the dog with "*Good* dog, Rambo!"

If the dog is told "No!" every time your son returns, the dog will associate the boy's homecoming with being scolded and will growl more and will be scolded more—and on and on. Or Rambo may be trying out some adolescent big-time dominance techniques. Your dog needs to be *taught (not punished)* that regardless of size, age or ego, your son is still ranks higher in the family pack.

Prevention: Kids need to know all the training words and techniques that the family dog has been taught and how to use them appropriately.

Question: "My dad says we'll have to get rid of my dog if she doesn't stop chewing. She is five months old (a Cocker Spaniel) and chews all the time. I want to keep her."

Answer: It's normal for pups to chew a lot while they're teething, and to some extent, dogs chew all their lives (see Chapter 7). Take an old towel, tie it in a knot, dampen it and put it in the fridge. When it's cold, play a very gentle game of tug-of-war down on the floor so the pup knows it is her toy. The rough towel will massage her gums and the cold will ease any pain of teething.

Prevention: Puppies "of all ages" can't chew up expensive possessions if they are confined to the safety of a kitchen or crate when no one is around to supervise their activities. (Show this to your dad so he'll know you're trying to be a responsible dog owner.)

Question: "My Cocker will ask to go out, but if it's raining she won't go out the door. This is a new problem; for six years rain never bothered her. If she doesn't go out, of course she has an accident. My parents are ready to send her to Never-Never Land!"

Answer: Retrain her. When she asks to go out, get into your raincoat, put on her leash, grab her favorite toy— and go out in the rain with a happy voice as if it were the most fun you've ever had. When she's about to relieve herself, cut the chatter and *as* she eliminates say Good dog. Go back inside immediately. Take her out just for fun whenever there's a light warm rainfall to help her overcome this rain phobia. Some dogs like the addition of a doggie raincoat. Be sure it's made of soft (noncrackling) fabric or you could be trading one fear (of getting wet) for another (noise).

Prevention: More older dogs than puppies object to the rain. Perhaps, like their owners, they just become more appreciative of creature comforts over the years.

Question: "The dog I grew up with died last year and my father says I can get a puppy now so long as I pay for any damage it does! My last dog was a female, and of course there was always the chance that she would get pregnant, but which makes a better pet, a male or a female?"

Answer: Let's take first things first. What you really want is a healthy, problem-free pet—therefore *a male should be neutered, a female spayed.* The personality or temperament depends first upon the breed or type of dog in general, then its inherited characteristics and third, the individual animal. You can add to all that the fact that some people simply prefer a male or a female for no particular reason.

Prevention: In acquiring a dog, you'll prevent disappointment down the line if you remember the universal warning: Look before you buy. When something about a puppy tells you it's the one for you, *be sure you've studied the breed,* met some adults of the breed and know more or less what to expect for the next ten to fifteen years. Then, have the pup spayed or neutered and enroll in a puppy kindergarten training class.

Question: "We are getting a puppy and my father says we have to keep her in a cage. My sister and I don't want to. Isn't it cruel?"

Answer: No, not at all. Dogs are "den" animals, which means they like to curl up in a small place where they feel safe and protected. It's her bed, so let the puppy sleep in the crate in your room so you'll hear her wake up and can take her outside on leash. You can have fun decorating the outside of the crate to look like a doll's bed with a pretty-canopy or a dust ruffle, so long as it's safe for the puppy.

Prevention: Crate training is the easiest and most reliable way to housetrain a puppy. The young puppy should be placed in (or lured into) the crate with a treat or toy until the pup will go in voluntarily, at first with the door left open. It's a good place for a pup to get away from loud family activities and enjoy a much-needed snooze. (See Chapter 1.)

Question: "My parents won't let me take my dog to Obedience class because she's too old. Buffie is seven. Is that too old? I'm eleven."

Answer: A dog is almost never too old to learn. Buffie will love all the attention if you make it fun. I hope you're lucky enough to find a class that's especially for kids.

Prevention: Youngsters should be wholeheartedly encouraged to attend school with their dogs. If nothing else, the experience will make them have some sympathy for their own classroom teachers. If money is a problem, there are even some trainers who give "scholarships," and in most areas of the country there are 4-H Extension Clubs that charge a minimal fee or nothing.

Question: "My nine-week-old Cocker puppy is not trained yet. She's okay at night, but when I take her out first thing in the morning all she wants to do is play. She races around and I can't catch her, and she doesn't go potty. Then she goes in the house and Mom gets mad at both of us!"

Answer: Take her outside *only* on leash so she can't race around. This is a "business trip," not playtime. Stay in one very small area until she eliminates, and say "Good girl" *as* she does. *Then* you can play! Always take her to the same place, and she'll soon catch on that when you walk over to that spot she should relieve herself before she can have fun or go back in the house.

Prevention: Housetraining is a high-priority problem in many new puppy households, and all it takes is a crate, a leash and one specific, acceptable bathroom area.

Question: "I have two dogs and they have one dog bed. The older dog, a female, won't let the male, Rap, get the bed. Why does he let her push him around?"

Answer: Your dogs have established their pack order, which they understand perfectly even if it doesn't always seem fair to you.

Prevention: It's normal behavior. Let them do it their way. A second bed for Rap might make you feel better, however.

Question: "I am ten years old and I can't take my dog for a walk because she is very strong, and as hard as I pull, she pulls harder. Only my Dad can walk her. What can I do?"

Answer: When the dog pulls, you should stop, call her back to your side in a happy voice and sometimes with a small treat. Tell her to sit, smile, praise her and then begin again. If you only take one step and she pulls, stop and repeat the whole routine again. Don't even try to outpull a dog! Keep the training sessions very short and always end by praising the dog. Keep smiling! You may have to work on it for several weeks before you can show off to your Dad.

Prevention: Teaching a dog to walk nicely without pulling begins the first time a puppy is asked to walk on a lead. With some pups it takes a lot of patience and practice. And then "suddenly" they catch on. Of course, it's not sudden at all. They just wise up and decide to do things *your* way.

Question: "We just adopted a Poodle mix about ten months old. My brother and I like him, but sometimes he nips at us when we're running and playing with him. How can we make him stop?"

Answer: The dog does not mean to bite. He's trying to play with you, but since he can't use hands as you do, he has to use teeth instead. Teach the dog to fetch a thrown toy, so before he gets too excited by your games, you can distract your dog by tossing one of his toys.

Prevention: When kids' play gets rough or noisy, dogs get a Time-out (in the house for a drink of water or a snooze) so nips don't turn into bites. No one should be punished, just separated. *Kids need to be taught not to wave their arms about,* or do too much running around a new dog (puppy or adopted) because to a dog those antics are an invitation to bite.

Question: "We have a Mini-Schnauzer puppy. What kind of toys should we get for him to play with?"

Answer: Toys are not just for play. Kids have certain educational toys, but for a dog *all* toys can have some instructional value. For instance, the puppy is caught

Some dogs are natural babysitters, and some babies don't at all mind being sat on.

chewing your shoe so you say "No" and replace it with a rawhide chew toy. The puppy barks after you say "stop," so you say "No bark" as you give a big soft toy to hold in his open mouth. Toys are used as distractions and rewards in teaching situations, which include games.

Prevention: The only caution about dog toys is the same as for toddlers: Be sure there are no small parts the pup can remove and swallow. Small puppies are fascinated by large toys.

Here are a few baby-related questions to end this chapter.

Question: "Boo-Boo is a six-year-old Shepherd mix and a VIP in the family. We are expecting our first baby, and it's imperative that baby and Boo live in harmony. How can I make it easier for Boo to share the spotlight?"

Answer: You've already got the right idea—the dog must learn to share. Let the dog participate in your preparations for the baby, but put a gate across the door to the baby's room so Boo will understand that admittance is by invitation only. Have your husband bring home from the hospital any piece of fabric that's been on the baby so the dog becomes familiar with the scent of this new person. When you attend to the baby, *let Boo go with you* using a Heel and Sit so your dog has a job to do. He'll soon get used to the baby sounds and smells, as well as the changes in your routine.

Prevention: Long before the baby arrives ease up a little on the attention given the dog so the dog has time to get used to not having one hundred percent of your time and focus.

Question: "I've got the terrible twos! My two-year-old dog, a Beagle, won't leave the baby's toys alone, and my two-year-old son won't stay out of the dog's water bowl. I thought this dog and baby bit was supposed to be fun!"

Answer: It can be fun if you keep your sense of humor and take charge. If Sonny doesn't heed your warning about the water bowl, give a Time-out. And do exactly the same thing with the dog. One warning "No," and if your warning is ignored, go to a Time-out.

Prevention: A short time in the clink (crib or crate) is boring and can do wonders to reinforce your authority and restore family peace. It's not punishment, it's discipline. Great for harried moms, too.

Question: "How should we introduce our totally spoiled Boxer to our new baby when we bring her home?"

Answer: First by scent *before* you come home, and then by letting the dog sniff and see the baby when you and baby arrive home.

Prevention: A boisterous dog should be allowed to greet Mom first because her strange hospital and baby scents will take some of the jump-up out of the dog. Then hold the baby in your lap for the dog to investigate. Avoid playing any form of "keep away," because the dog will not understand your intention and think you are teasing. Teased dogs will always try to grab the elusive object. Let your dog sniff, look, nuzzle and sniff some more.

Speak when you're spoken to,
Do as you're told,
Wag your tail after you,
COME! when you're called.

—Victoriana Askew

11

THE VALUE OF OBEDIENCE

The subject of Obedience training always seems to come up regardless of what other delights or pitfalls about dog ownership are being discussed. That's because *Obedience training of some kind is essential,* not only to responsible dog ownership, but to the full enjoyment of the dog. By itself, however, it does not, it cannot, solve problems. It forms the basis of a partnership, giving you and your dog a concise working language. Since it's natural for pet owners to be overly verbal with their dogs, defeating that concept, the first rule of Obedience training is "One command and one response." That's mostly for the dog. The owner has another first rule, which is "Don't nag. Teach."

Dog and owner learn to understand one another, forging the communication link that allows the owner to teach the dog everything from safety to good manners to stupid pet tricks.

A dog's world consists of leaders and followers. You must be one or the other. The dog takes on whichever vacancy is up for grabs. If you are not a good leader, Rufus will immediately take over because the way he looks at it, "Someone's got to do it!"

There is a current debate that questions how much, *if any,* dominance anyone should exert over a dog. Unfair, harsh, angry, abusive dominance is certainly way out of line. In a dog it's called being dominant-aggressive and is unacceptable behavior. It's equally unacceptable in people.

Our pets do not mature beyond adolescence, and we are their providers and protectors for life, so it is essential to maintain the same kind of parental guidance given a child. You hold a toddler's hand; you walk the dog on a leash. A toddler left home alone all day would get into about as much trouble as the dog. (Granted, the dog, with animal skills intact, might be more inventively destructive.) So no matter what the label—Alpha, Top Dog, Leader, Dominant Partner or Parent—the owner is responsible for the physical and mental health and the behavior of the dog for its lifetime, and that includes instruction.

Teaching a dog all the Obedience commands would be a waste of time and money if they were only meant to be used in class. It would be like teaching little Sara the alphabet, but not how to read. Once you and the dog know the language, *use* it every day. That language is the "tool" with which *you* can prevent so many common problems. In fact, there are lots of behavioral problems that could be helped, solved or better yet prevented by some formal Obedience training.

OBEDIENCE—GREAT FOR DOGS AND PEOPLE TOO!

Question: "We adopted a dog from a local shelter, and the people there suggested we attend the Obedience classes they give. My husband thinks it's a gimmick to get more money from those who take dogs off their hands. Wouldn't a book from the library be just as good?"

Answer: First, let me explain about the shelter staff. Many are dedicated volunteers. They are undertaking the monumental job of correcting the problems that landed the dogs in the shelter in the first place. In addition, they are going to try to teach good people like you who have adopted the unwanted dogs. Believe me, this is no get-rich-quick scheme!

You and your husband will learn two important things in a class. One is the one-word verbal communication mentioned previously, which you *can* learn from a book. The other is timing. *When* to correct, *when* to show how or *when* to praise a dog is every bit as important as *how* you do it. A book cannot correct *you* when your timing is off and you are not getting the right message across to your dog. Also, a book does not offer your dog a chance to learn in the presence of other dogs.

Prevention: Grab those classes offered for adopted dogs!

Question: "My dog is an angel at home, but makes a fool of me in class. The instructor wasn't concerned, but I was. I quit!"

Answer: It's a common complaint, and the reverse situation is just as prevalent: the dog is near perfect in class and couldn't care less about homework. In either case, stick to it! Don't let the dog dictate what she will or will not do. If the instructor wasn't upset, it would seem the situation is more of an embarrassment to you than a problem with the dog.

Prevention: Lighten up and keep it fun, or at least interesting for the Obedience cutup. Know, too, that a previously "perfect" dog may not be so flawless when going through his teenage phase (around ten to twelve months of age). Stick to your guns—and trust me, down the road some of the foolish schoolroom antics will be among the most treasured memories of your pet.

Question: "All I want to teach my Labrador Retriever is not to jump up on every person who comes near her. Will Obedience school teach her that?"

Answer: No. But it will teach *you* how to teach her! Begin with absolute consistency in all commands. (That does *not* mean repeating "Off" a hundred times a day!) Put her on a Sit/Stay *every* time someone approaches. Your long-term goal is to have the dog sit without being told when anyone is about to say hello. (Tail wagging is a very acceptable embellishment.) This training takes patience, especially with a friendly, outgoing Lab.

Obedience is a great way to socialize your dog. It's a great way to meet people, too.

Prevention: With a dog that will be large at maturity, start teaching the Sit/Stay (or Stand) the first time puppy tries to balance on her back feet begging to be petted. The dog is greeted or petted *only* when she has four-on-the-floor.

Everyone in the household must use the same friendly command, enforcing it every time. (That's what's meant by consistency.) This includes all family members. Kids, too. Rules are rules. It's better to teach the Sit/Stay because it's easier to enforce, than to say an ineffective "Off" over and over to a hundred pounds of friendly bouncing fur. Some people prefer to have the dog stand, but it is often harder to teach than the Sit.

Question: "I've never taken a dog to Obedience school, and all my dogs have been well behaved. Not one has ever caused me a moment's problem."

Answer: You must be a gifted teacher, and extremely lucky in your choice of dogs. Not many dogs or owners are so blessed.

Prevention: Albert Schweitzer once said that good health is a lot of luck, and a poor memory. Perhaps a doggie version of this maxim is also true?

Question: "My Obedience class wore me out. Everyone already knew what to do, there was never time to ask questions and all anyone ever talked about were Trials and titles!"

Answer and Prevention: Oops! You entered "college" by mistake! Always visit two or three sessions without your dog before signing up. Pay attention to find out if you understand at least some of what's going on, whether or not most handlers are beginners like you and how the instructor deals with problems (dogs, owners and questions).

Begin with puppy kindergarten if your pup is under five months of age. If that's not available, or your dog is older, go for Obedience classes that have a Canine Good Citizen award as the ultimate goal, not competitive trial events. If you start at the right level, you will enjoy working with your dog. You might even be bitten by the competitive bug, so don't throw out that canine college address yet.

Dog trainers are wisely beginning to classify their schools so owners can tell which one best suits their needs. At the present time, however, most classes are divided only according to the dogs' ability: Beginners, Pre-Novice, Novice, etc. This does not indicate the level of the handler's skill, so the first-time pet owner's morale is understandably crushed in a beginners class full of beginner dogs, but with very experienced handlers.

Question: "My dog did very well in Obedience training, but the confusion of cars, trucks and people outdoors is more than he can take. He's still a lunging lunatic when we walk on the street."

Answer: This is called a "situation excuse." It's easier to blame the people, trucks and cars than to accept the fact that an otherwise well-behaved dog has to be taught to handle stress conditions. Ask your instructor for additional work on heeling with distractions, or do it on your own.

Begin at a time of day when there's a minimum of traffic and people. (Sunday in a school parking lot?) Keep the session brief and cheerful. Better to go half a short block and go home than to end up in a tug-of-war with a stressed-out dog. You might want to switch from an ordinary training collar to one of the anti-pull devices such as the Halti head collar or the No-Pull harness available through pet supply stores and catalogs.

Prevention: Use leadership, not excuses. Puppies naturally *follow,* but they can't do it if there is no leader!

Question: "I've been taking my Basset Hound to training classes, but my boyfriend is impatient with her constant begging for food. I feel we need to wait until we've completed the course before expecting her not to beg. It hasn't been covered in class yet."

Answer: This is yet another dog-owner maneuver to shift the blame or the cause of the unacceptable behavior. A dog doesn't have to go to school to learn not to beg! *You* decide where you want the dog to be during meals or snacks—the dog's bed, for example, and teach the dog the one-word command "Bed!"

Then, before you begin to eat anything at all, whether it's a full meal or a TV snack, send the dog to its place. Ignore! Do not look at or speak to the dog. This is not a punishment. It's discipline.

Prevention: In many of these cases of disobedience, Prevention is as easy as: **Don't blame the dog and don't make excuses!**

Question: "Our puppy is eight months old. He's just a pet so I figure why should I spend time and money on Obedience training. My husband agrees that dogs just pick up what they need to know."

Answer: Read about the problems discussed on every page in this book and I think you'll change your mind. "Just a pet" is not a valid excuse for denying your dog an education. In fact, it's a *primary reason* for training!

Prevention: See previous Prevention.

Question: "My dad says because of the cost I can only take the puppy to one Obedience course (eight weeks). Is that enough?"

Answer: No, not really, but it is better than nothing at all. Pay attention, do your homework (have fun doing it), graduate at the head of your class and, who knows, maybe the trainer will give you a scholarship! Or Dad may have a change of heart.

Prevention: The cost of Obedience training should be figured in with the other initial expenses when getting a dog—veterinary fees for the first checkup and immunizations, a crate, quality food, collar and leash, food and water dishes, toys *and* training. Parents should look into 4-H Extension Services. Some offer free instruction, and Obedience courses given through Adult Education are often fairly inexpensive as well. Only attending one course of instruction is akin to quitting school after first grade.

Question: "I have no intention of getting involved in competition, so what use is Obedience school except to make my dog learn a few commands? I have no desire to be a Marine sergeant."

Answer: I hardly know where to begin! Those commands are merely tools for you to *use*. It's raining, you don't feel like going for a long walk but Rufus needs some exercise, so let him help with the housework. Teach your dog to carry a basket of your cleaning needs from room to room (or concoct a custom-made saddlebag). Use Sit, Take It and Give It to turn your dog into an uncomplaining, non-critical cleaning partner. Heel and Sit/Stay, followed by Come, will let you go through doors first. No matter what the breed, you've now got yourself a true "working" dog.

You are using Obedience commands as they are meant to be used—in normal everyday life.

Prevention: *Obedience training teaches you how to teach your dog.* After that, your imagination's the limit!

Question: "My dog follows me around everywhere and it drives me nuts. How can I make her stop? Yelling hasn't worked."

Answer: Some dogs are more social or anxious to please than others. (Slaves is more like it.) Is it possible that you are actually encouraging the dog to follow you by grumbling or yelling too much? Those are all forms of

After basic training, the sky's the limit.

verbal attention to a dog. Go for a short, brisk walk so your dog gets some exercise and companionship. Then say "Crate" or "Bed" with a big smile, add a toy or treat for a good dog and ignore her. No peeking, no talking.

Prevention: Basic crate training to the rescue! When you need time by yourself, give the dog a crate break, but without anger. The dog is not being punished, just doing as she's been told. Definitely a Good Dog.

Question: "My Tibetan Terrier, Tibby, is very smart and did extremely well in training. We have only one problem, and it is more of a mystery than a misbehavior. When she's out in the yard and we call 'Come' she wags her whole rear end but remains stock still! We end up having to go out and pick her up. What's going on here?"

Answer: Somewhere along the line Tibby confused "Come" with "Stay" and, since you go to collect her, she now figures she must have it right! Start over again, on lead, teaching her to come by using a completely different word, for example, "Tibby, *Here!*" Even more important than the word you use is your body language. Crouch down, arms outspread and a huge smile on your face. Sound really excited. Keep her on lead so you can control those four-wheel brakes!

Prevention: Dogs also learn from every incorrect signal we give them. Sometimes it seems they learn these things even more quickly!

Question: "My dog always wants to be part of the conversation, and it's no longer funny. Friends come over and the minute we sit down to talk, the dog sounds off. How can I tell him to be quiet without also interrupting whoever is talking?"

Answer: This one is easy! Teach your dog a hand signal. Just a forefinger to the mouth, the same signal you'd use to ask anyone to be quiet. At first, you'll have to accompany it with your verbal command, but gradually change over to just the silent silencer.

Prevention: Hand signals can be taught right along with verbal commands for the very reason that dogs "read" our body language. It's a neat way to teach the dog to do tricks, too.

Never be caught without a plan. Know exactly
what you'd do if someone gave you a million dollars,
or took your last dime, or stole your dog.

—Aunt Meg's Golden Rule

12

LITTLE DOG LOST

No matter what the *actual* size of a dog, a lost dog is a little dog. Scared, pathetic, bewildered, needy—"little." Typically trotting along the road, looking up expectantly at every car hurtling by, in an attempt to retain some semblance of dignity, lost dogs often put on an air of "I know where I'm going." Only they don't. They are the embodiment of the stereotypical person who won't ask for directions!

We have been romanced into thinking lost dogs have a sixth sense bordering on the miraculous because of all the wonderful tales of Lassie, Charlie, et al. Once in a great while on the TV evening news we see the happy reunion of a dog that found its way from one place to another hundreds of miles away. Just keep in mind *why* you are viewing it on your screen: Because it *is* so rare, it makes news! Those stories capture our hearts because they share the happy ending that we *want* for every lost dog, but sadly they are not even close to the norm.

Realistically, dogs that become lost seldom find their own way home and only *sometimes* are found. Dogs can't read signs.

They don't know when they have crossed from one town into another or one county into another, and that the street outside their home is nothing like the superhighway now facing them. But that's unfair. It begins to sound as if I'm putting the blame on the dogs themselves for being lost. Not so. It's the owners who don't take into account the pet's view of topography and town boundaries in our confusing world.

RESPONSIBILITY

Responsible dog owners provide fences and leashes as safety measures against their dogs ever becoming lost, but dogs dig their way out, leashes break, and doors and gates do not always close securely. These things happen to the best of owners and the best of dogs. It is not a perfect world.

What's a pet owner to do? There are lots of easy things you can do to be prepared should catastrophe strike. Set up a Rufus Emergency File (be it an envelope or shoe box) in which you put:

- A recent, clear, close-up snapshot of Rufus. One head shot and one body shot would be even better.
- Dog license—i.e., The piece of paper. (The tag, along with a rabies tag, should be *on* Rufus, on a regular collar, not a choke or training collar.)
- Tattoo registry number.
- Health record—everything from the veterinarian.
- Telephone numbers: Your vet; tattoo registry; every canine control officer, every shelter (public and private) in a twenty-five- to fifty-mile radius; any training instructor, groomer, boarding kennel, dog club or similar affiliation you may have. If the dog is purebred, add the numbers of the breeder and the breed rescue person nearest you. Add anyone else who might be supportive in the search. (In an emergency, phone numbers are easily forgotten.)

People who are involved in dogs, especially those in your breed, will be more concerned and anxious to help look for a lost dog than the police or dog wardens, who may promise to notify you when and if Rufus is found (but don't count on it). These town or city officials can't spend the time (time is money) searching for lost pets.

The Answers to the following Questions will show you a number of ways to use the contents of your Rufus Emergency File in searching for your "little" lost dog.

Question: "Three summers ago our dog got lost while we were camping out of state. He was never found. How can we protect our new dog, a two-year-old Collie, when we go camping this year?"

Answer: Make copies of most of the papers in your emergency file and take them with you. Check your dog's collar and leash to be certain they are not worn or frayed, and pack an extra new set anyway. Don't rely on "Rufus, come!" when you're on strange turf; your dog may be tuned in to something entirely different. *Use the leash.* Use a tie-out stake *only* when you are right there, but need your two hands on the "barbie" or some such. If you use a tie-out when you are not present, all kinds of trouble can befall your dog, including self-injury, attack by other animals or people and theft.

Prevention: Dogs that "never wander off" *do*. Check the latches on your RV door and screen door and always teach the dog, long before the trip, to Wait and let any human member of the family go through a door first. (That's manners used as a Prevention.) *All these things help to prevent a dog from becoming lost or stolen.*

Question: "When we stopped for gas on the highway, our dog jumped out of the car and then raced off into woods behind the gas station. We were about a hundred and fifty miles from home and had to keep going. There seemed to be nothing we could do, but the whole family was broken up about it. Was there anything we could have done? We all hope someone found our dog and gave him a good home."

Answer: This is especially tough on kids who may see the same kind of thing happening to them—lost and abandoned! You can still take action even when you must

A lost dog is a sad and soulful sight and may fall victim to many dangers.

continue your journey. Call the local police and the area canine control officer and give them as much information as you can about the dog plus your home phone number and address. (Brownie points for asking them to call you collect.)

If the gas station attendant is from the area, give the same information plus a snapshot of the dog (which you, of course, keep in the glove compartment). Ask that the photo be posted by the cash register. Chat with the attendant, who may know who lives on the other side of the woods, or some such, and if so, get the name and telephone number. Get the name of the local paper and phone in an ad when you get home. Offer a reward. Putting a monetary value on the dog may stimulate the search.

When you get home, call your Tattoo Registry and your breeder or breed rescue person. These people will get on the case instantly and usually have a network in place (unless you happened to have been in Death Valley).

Prevention: Every dog that rides in a motor vehicle needs a safety device, be it a crate, a securely installed barrier or a canine seat belt. It is law in two states (California and Oregon) at present. Regardless of the size or age of your dog, think "toddler" and follow similar safety precautions.

Question: "When our Sheltie ran away, we notified the nearby elementary school because Posie loves kids. Friends said it was a dumb thing to do, but it worked! A young girl brought Posie back."

Answer: That was a very smart thing to do. School children are great tracers of lost dogs, partly because dogs do tend to gravitate toward playgrounds. In rural areas, post flyers (with a picture) at as many school bus stops as you can. Local radio stations usually announce lost and found pets. Alert all the delivery people in your area because they are apt to know the dogs on their route and would spot a familiar face that pops up in the wrong place.

Prevention: Hang on to clear pictures of your dog and be quick to circulate huge-lettered, simply-worded flyers. Put them up so they can be read by the driver of a car, and post them in supermarkets, shopping centers and pet shops. (Remember to remove them when Rufus is found!) The proliferation of copy machines makes this one of the least expensive ways to get the word out that Rufus is missing.

Question: "Some people found my German Shorthaired Pointer running around a mall parking lot, but no one could get close enough to grab her collar. She is a bit shy, but it even took three hours before she'd come to me! Is it possible to train a dog like that to respond to anyone who might have to give her a command?"

Answer: Maybe, for example, if you had started the training when she was twelve weeks old, but the chances of turning her around now are slim. If it took three hours for her to come to you, I'd say she's more than "a bit" shy or she has a real problem with the meaning of "Come!"

Basically, there are three methods to try when dealing with a skittish lost dog. One is to leave a worn (owner-scented) article of clothing with a few dog biscuits tucked inside, where the dog was seen in the hope that it will return to that spot. Then monitor the area for as many hours as you can. This is called "patience." Another method is to use a Have-A-Heart trap baited with any food the dog particularly likes. This is called "entrapment." Then there is the last resort—the "flying tackle" (not recommended for parking lots), which is only to be used when all else fails.

Prevention: Breed specifics can determine the method used to capture a lost dog that's been sighted. Breeds that are generally aloof *or* shy with strangers (Borzois, Afghans, Pointers, Basenjis, Shelties and most of the Herding dogs, among them) are the most difficult to recover. Dogs that are natural prey-chasers (Terriers or sighthounds, for instance) can sometimes be captured by calling and running away from the dog, inciting a chase.

Chow hounds might be coaxed into approaching any person armed with hot dogs, hamburger or other good-smelling treats. Any dog that loves a car ride will hop right in when your car door is open. This can backfire (pun intended). A dog that will jump into anyone's car is easily stolen. Teach your dog a specific command for getting into a car with you and then proof-train this by trying to urge the dog into your car with words other than the correct one. Lots of praise for getting this lesson right.

Question: "Our dog keeps running away and hasn't any idea how to get home. Sometimes she goes as much as ten miles on these jaunts. Which is better, to drive around the neighborhood calling for the lost dog, or just to stay in the house and phone everyone we can think of?"

Answer: It's a mistake to drive around the neighborhood calling from the car as you go. By the time the dog hears you and runs to where your call came from, you could be two miles in another direction. Cover nearby turf on foot with the help of friends first, then get in the car and go further away but keep stopping to park the car and stay in each spot for several minutes before moving on. And don't call just before pulling out. If someone can stay home making calls or waiting for the phone to ring, that's your best bet, but if not, check your answering machine.

Prevention: *You need a good leash and a strong fence!* The best prevention is one that ensures the dog will not be able to take these jaunts.

Question: "I feel guilty because when I found Bridge-It, I didn't do enough to reunite her with her real owner. She was running in traffic on a highway bridge and hopped in my car when I opened the door. She had no collar and no I.D. I kept looking in the papers, but never saw an ad for a lost dog that came even close to what she looks like. What else could I have done? She has not given me a minute's trouble. A perfect pet!"

Answer: You could have checked with the shelters, pounds, police, etc., but it's possible that Bridge-It (what an appropriate name!) hopped out of her owner's car as neatly as she hopped into yours and the owner had no idea where or when it happened. Lucky you.

Prevention: Seat belts! Crates! Fences, leashes, barriers! Identification!

Question: "What should I do when my lost dog returns? Would your answer be different if the dog returned on his own or was brought back by the finder?"

Answer: There is only one answer: Jump for joy! Let the dog know in every way you can that this is the happiest of moment of your life. Smiles, hugs, cookies, ice cream, steak . . . lay it on!

Prevention: All of the previous advice will help prevent a dog from becoming lost a second time, along with **a leash, a fence, closed doors, crates, etc.**

Question: "Our suburban area is often the target of dog and cat thieves. Is there anything we can do to protect our pets? Should I train my dogs to attack strangers?"

Answer: Training a pet to be an attack dog is a poor idea. You'd be living with a time bomb, and besides, very few dogs have the temperament and intelligence to be trained for such complicated and disciplined work. Keep your cats indoors and walk the dogs on leash. Fences are good deterrents but don't offer one hundred percent protection from dognappers. *Electronic or unseen fences just make the thieves' job too easy.*

Prevention: Set up a neighborhood watch for unmarked vans. Get the license plate number. Stop vans that appear to be cruising and ask what address they're looking for. If they speed off, or you hear dogs inside, call the police.

Question: "I'm always afraid my dog will get lost, because if he does, it would be impossible to get him back. He never comes when called!"

Answer: Obedience training gives owners the tools for safety, one of which is the establishment of trust. A dog that has been scolded or punished for *not* coming when called won't take a chance when lost or frightened because this dog cannot trust the owner not to punish him.

Prevention: Teach your dog that the one and only response to "Come!" is a *Good dog joyous reunion,* even if he's been bad and needs a slight tug on the leash to remind him, even if at first he also gets cheese and crackers, twenty times a day if need be! *Please!* Because I've just about run out of Preventions for this one!

Question: "I live year round in a summer resort area. Every September we have to cope with all the cats and dogs that are left behind when the summer people return to the city. They get these pets for their kids the way they buy beach balls. Most of them are completely untrained, undisciplined dogs."

Answer: This end-of-season abandonment occurs in most, if not all, areas with summer residents. It's unacceptable because it is premeditated, and worse because it teaches the next generation of parents and dog owners that the life of a pet has no value, that it's okay to be a throwaway society.

Prevention: Pet adoption agencies could set up rules that would screen out adoptions by "summer people." One of the primary reasons to get a dog for a child is to teach such values as long-term caring, sharing and responsibility. It's what parenting is all about. Throughout the summer the year-round residents could involve these kids in pet education programs just as is being done in many public schools. Keep it fun and they'll come.

Question: "A dog was lurking around our house for weeks before she would come near us. We left food out and the dog would steal it and run off. She had a collar, but no tags. When we 'captured' the dog and brought her indoors, she was terrified. The vet prescribed medication for a time which calmed her a little, but the dog is still supersensitive. How can we help?"

Answer: When a dog like this is finally caught, the "umbilical cord" method works well. Put her on a long leash and tie the other end to your belt so she has to go everywhere and learn everything with you. Take the dog out on a very strong leash and hang on! Be extremely careful to keep outside doors closed. Time will be the ultimate healer of your distraught dog.

Prevention: Since the dog was wearing a collar, it was not a feral animal, but one that obviously had not been having an easy time of it. The scars of trauma are often the most difficult to erase.

Question: "Our dog got himself lost and my son found him in the pound, where we had to pay to get the dog back. I think he's a stupid dog. Is there any way to put some sense in his head?"

Answer: You've hit on one of my pet peeves. The dog did *not* "get *himself* lost." He became lost when *your safety net failed!* Mend your fences. Check the collars and leashes. Sign up for training classes. The dog is probably much smarter than you imagine. Reread this chapter.

Prevention: Putting all the blame on the dog is a neat way to get out of taking the responsibility, or having to cope with feelings of guilt, but dogs do not set out purposely to "get lost," no matter how often we may say it in jest.

13

MOST OFTEN ASKED QUESTIONS

The questions pet owners ask about their dogs' behavior almost always tie in with the owners' perception of what is acceptable *family* behavior and what is not. In our culture, dogs kept as pets (as opposed to the very few gainfully employed working dogs) do live as members of the family and are expected to toe the line.

Of course, no matter what the behavior—good, bad or indifferent—it is perfectly acceptable to the dog. There are perks. The dog benefits from whatever leeway exists within the confines of family life. If the kids are allowed to jump on furniture, the dog can, too (and does). If everyone eats between meals, you can bet that Rufus is wherever the food is. A rowdy household begets a rowdy dog. And so on.

That's fine with everyone so long as the dog's behavior is in sync with the rules and regulations of the family. What is generally regarded as problem behavior is more likely to be just "dog" pure and simple. It is seen as a problem by the owner (again, not by the dog) because when all is said and done, that adorable pet is an animal, of the wonderful canine persuasion, but an animal nevertheless. The result is a pristine dwelling with a dog to match (no room for error) or it won't have a pet at all. Allowed to do so, Rufus would do things his way.

Of course, what most dog owners fail to realize is that anything the puppy does today he will do again tomorrow and tomorrow unless shown how to do it differently. It's not like dealing with a toddler who will "outgrow" unwanted behavior (or come in line with maturity.) To a puppy, forever is now. So dog owners themselves may inadvertently *teach* the dog many of the things they later find unacceptable, because to Rufus, if you allow it, it must be okay.

These behaviors that are overlooked in a young pup all too soon become excessive and uncontrollable. If you praise your puppy for giving you a bouncing, jumping, enthusiastic greeting, keep in mind that only a few months from now at 110 pounds, the same greeting will be a battle for equilibrium! So you may change the rules—but Rufus retains the imprint of the first one. Seeing puppy chewing on her rawhide or the corner of her own blanket is like watching a baby with a pacifier or security blanket. But how quickly it loses all its charm when the item being chewed is your leather jacket! These two activities rank high on the list of Most Common Complaints.

There are more: Why does the dog dig up my flowers? Why does Buster never bark in the daytime, but keep the neighbors awake all night? Why did the puppy throw up on the new carpet?

The one answer to all these complaints is: This is a dog and needs to be taught *what behavior is acceptable under your roof.* All these things are "species correct" and without our moral or material values. A dog that is punished or scolded, hearing "No" from morning till night, only learns that his name seems to have been changed from Rufus to No. (Test it. In a sweet, enticing voice, call "No, where are you?")

TEACH AND YOUR DOG SHALL LEARN

Lack of education is the real problem; undesirable behavior is merely the result. Barking, digging, chewing and biting are all things that normal dogs do and that their owners complain about. Dogs also shed, shake when wet, don't always come when called, bring home "gifts" of dead birds, throw up anywhere they happen to be and leave muddy footprints on clean floors!

Some of these things are covered in other chapters devoted specifically to the individual topic, but are included again here—perhaps in a slightly different version—because they rank high among the Most Common Questions.

Question: "Our dog is five years old and completely housebroken, but she always pees when anyone goes to pet her or talk to her. My husband whacks her with a rolled-up newspaper. I scold and correct her but nothing does any good. The vet says there is nothing wrong with her physically. Why does she do this?"

Answer: Your dog is not being naughty or disobedient. What you describe is called "submissive urination," which is a behavioral problem, not a physical one. Some dogs roll over on their backs to indicate submission. Some do both—roll over and urinate. Punishment is the worst thing you can do because the dog will try harder to be *more* submissive! (More peeing.) It's easier to change this particular behavior in a puppy than an older dog, but the Prevention below may help.

Prevention: The submissive or shy dog must be allowed to greet people on its own terms and in its own good time. Do not reach out to pet such a dog when you are standing up or bending over it. That's a dominant posture to which the dog will react submissively. (More urinating.) Friends and family can help by ignoring the dog.

Question: "Our two dogs are outside all day when we're at work and indoors when we're home. The problem is that the male urinates in different places throughout the house overnight. I've tried various cleaning products, but it doesn't help."

Answer: He is marking territory—saying loud and clear in dog-ese, "This house is *my* house." Clean the areas with one of the excellent new products made for the purpose. Regular household products won't do it. Confine the dog to one room (the kitchen perhaps?) and use a verbal distraction when you see him sniff or about to lift a leg. Crate your dog overnight.

Prevention: Marking territory is as normal to a male dog as breathing. It is not house soiling. An outside dog is never scolded for it, that is, *until* he comes indoors and continues his natural outdoor behavior. Observe or confine.

Question: "What's the point of crate training a puppy?"

Answer: The question should be (and the answer definitely is) plural! There are numerous points to crate training. The benefits for the dog, the owner and everyone involved in caring for your dog would make a long, long list.

Prevention: A crate-trained dog always has a place that is her very own and where she is always a Good dog. The phrase "crate training" does not, as many people mistakenly think, only refer to housebreaking a puppy. That's just one of many uses. Once crate trained, a dog will accept being put in a crate no matter who is in charge—the owner, groomer, vet, boarding kennel staff, etc. The dog has learned that in the crate she is safe and secure, has your approval and can relax. When used for a Time-out, the crate remains a safe haven. The message the dog gets is more of an "oops" than yet another "No, bad dog."

Question: "I hate to even say this, but my dog has a disgusting habit—she eats poop. No amount of yelling at her stops it. I'm mortified. What can I do?"

Answer: Forget about being mortified and stop yelling. This is another topic high on the "why?" list. It is just another activity that proves that a pet dog, despite all our efforts to change it, is still an animal. Unless your dog has a worm infestation (check with your vet), eating its own feces will not harm the dog. We consider it disgusting, but the dog does not, so if you look at it that way, it's our problem and not the dog's.

Prevention: Take the dog out *on leash* to eliminate and pick up the feces immediately. And yes, you *can* train your dog to go while on a leash! (Another common complaint.) Separate this "business trip" from a walk and all it takes is a little time and patience.

Question: "Why is my great big German Shepherd Dog terrified of thunder, motorcycles and fireworks?"

Answer: Self-preservation is the simple answer, and it applies to dogs of all sizes and breeds. You may have unintentionally fed the dog's fear by the way *you* handled it the first time. (See Chapter 5 for more on fears.)

Prevention: Treat noises casually. Do not coddle, cuddle, coo at, pick up or verbally comfort a puppy that shows any sign of fear. Your casual attitude will be a cue as to how the pup should also react. It's the old "whistle a happy tune" method—and it works.

No matter how many times the owner tried to teach this trick, Bucky would not go down the slide. Not every dog is an Olympic athlete.

Question: "My dog has been to a very good Obedience school, but still won't come when I call him. It is so frustrating to keep shouting and have him pay no attention to me."

Answer: You should have stayed after school. Remember the rule? **One command, one response.** Don't nag. Teach. And always on leash so you can teach the correct response. No shouting. Get the dog's attention, then give the command. Reinforce the positive response with a smile, a pat, a treat, or a "Good dog."

Prevention: Stay in school long enough to "proof" your dog, that is, to teach that he must *always,* under any and all circumstances no matter what the distractions, obey "Come" immediately. Obviously, you have committed the ultimate error of saying "Come" when the dog was off lead and could disobey you. Then you got mad and the dog got smart: "Stay away from people who are angry," he said to himself, "and they always get angry when they say that word, "Come!"

Question: "Our dog used to be quiet outside but now barks all night. How can we stop this? The neighbors complain."

Answer: Something about being outside is bothering the dog and you could spend many more sleepless nights trying to figure out what it is. The easiest way to stop it is to bring the dog inside. House dogs seldom bark all night. At least not more than once!

Prevention: Dogs are *social* animals in need of companionship. Dogs that are relegated to a solitary existence outdoors day and night are generally uneducated and unsocialized, a combination that signifies neglect. Teach your dog how to behave in the house so he can be a part of the family. He will probably be a better watchdog for knowing firsthand what he's protecting.

Question: "Why do you so often suggest Obedience training for dogs with problems? I don't want a dog that is a slave or a robot, just well behaved at home and with friends."

Answer: Dogs are individuals. Some do have a need to be slaves but relatively few become robots from attending school. Obedience classes teach owners how to get their dogs to behave nicely "at home and with friends." People who skip school are apt to have dogs that get into trouble. By the way, I also often point out that *it's the owner who has the problem,* not the dog!

Prevention: Obedience-educated dogs and owners run into fewer problems than those who try to get by without training.

Question: "Our dog attended puppy kindergarten classes and got along with all the other dogs and people. Now, out of the blue, he has started acting shy and fearful even with people he knows. Did we do something to cause this?"

Answer: You didn't cause it, but you may be reinforcing it. Most pups go through a "fear phase" at around five months of age. Don't *do* anything! That means don't push the pup on people; don't let others try to overcome the fear with too much well-intended attention; don't try sweet-talking; don't make any unusual demands on the dog during this stage. Remain cheerful and matter-of-fact.

Prevention: Be prepared for a fear phase in puppies at about five months of age. Avoid new experiences that might prove frightening and sudden loud noises (lawn mowers or similar loud machinery). Some pups go through it in a few days, some take a couple of weeks. Being casual and good-natured helps to speed up the process. Commiserating will prolong it.

Question: "Our first Miniature Schnauzer was easy to train and was a perfect gentleman until his dying day—at the age of fifteen. Six months ago we bought another Mini-Schnauzer puppy and it has been disaster all the way. I can't believe that two dogs of the same breed could be so totally different. He gets into everything, still is not housebroken and pulls my wife down the street. I could go on and on. Has the breed changed that much in twenty years?"

Answer: The breed hasn't changed, but no doubt you have! It is human nature to have a selective memory, which helps you conveniently forget all the problems you encountered before the first dog settled down to fit your family like a comfortable old pair of slippers. Personal possessions may have more sentimental or monetary value to you now. If you are not crate training this pup, you are missing a great opportunity to make life easier. It wasn't a popular concept with pet owners fifteen or twenty years ago.

Prevention: No one should ever take on a dog of any age thinking that it is going to be like the previous dog. Little things may remind you of the former dog, but leave yourself open to all the new joys and pleasures of this one.

Question: "No matter how many times I've whacked the puppy for messing in the house, she continues to do it. I'm about ready to give her back to the shelter. What else can I do?"

Answer: Stop whacking. It may make you feel better, but *it does not teach* the pup where she should and should not eliminate. **Teach, don't punish.** Begin again at the beginning. (See Chapter 1.)

Prevention: Physical punishment is counterproductive. Even when caught in the act of misbehaving, a puppy should be given the smallest correction needed to stop it immediately and completely. Every correction must then be followed by teaching the desired behavior.

Question: "We got an Australian Cattle Dog as a young pup and he has become everything we ever wanted in a dog— except. Except at fourteen months of age he has started lifting his leg when we visit friends and relatives, even in the vet's office. Is this a "forever" problem? If not, how do I get my super-dog back?"

Answer: Your puppy grew up, that's all. Now he's telling the world that he was here, and here, and here, and here! Neutering will sometimes reduce a male dog's instinct to mark territory, but it is not a sure cure. Keep your dog on leash when you go visiting, watch him closely and use **Prevention, not punishment.**

Prevention: The time to prevent "marking" is when the dog first sniffs prior to lifting a leg. *That's* when you shout a distraction such as "Acht!" (That's a "don't-even-think-it." Save "No" for a "stop-whatever-you're-doing.") Follow it instantly with mild praise and give the dog something else to do, like lie down at your feet.

Question: "We recently adopted a two-year-old male mixed-breed. The problem is he steals all the toys, food, etc., from our other (smaller) dog and has bitten me when I've tried to take things away from him. He's okay about any of these things if I happen to get there first, but once it's in his mouth, forget it!"

Answer: It's that age-old law of possession. Get this dog into Obedience class so you can establish yourself as leader of your pack. This problem calls for a Sit/Stay, Take it, Give it routine. A trick for getting a dog to give it graciously is to offer a slice of hot dog (or any preferred super-treat) in one hand as you accept the object in the other.

Prevention: Adopted older dogs do not come with clean slates. They have many, many adjustments to make. Obedience classes, combined with lots of friendly practice at home, make the transition less stressful.

Question: "How can I get my King Charles Spaniel to stop pawing at me? She is an adorable dog, but the pawing when I'm reading, watching TV, talking to friends, etc., drives me nuts!"

Answer: Pawing is an excellent attention-getter. (It gets yours!) Note that she does this when you are otherwise engaged or not paying attention to your adorable dog. Try Ignoring first, with an occasional Time-out for emphasis.

Prevention: Pawing ranges from annoying to destructive depending on the size of the dog, its nails and its determination. Puppies paw litter mates and adult dogs to get attention. They find it works well on people, too! Since it's not a behavior the pup will outgrow, it should be stopped the first time. Enforce "Off" followed by Ignoring. (You know why that is capitalized, right? See pages 16, 47 and 50.)

Question: "My English Springer Spaniel pulls me down the street every day. I've tried the snap-and-release collar correction but it doesn't work when the dog is pulling so hard against the collar. I have tried pulling back and scolding, but nothing does any good. Have you any suggestions?"

Answer: The cure will also test your patience, but here is one way. When the dog pulls, make a nasty "Acht!" sound, stop and bring him back beside you, preferably in a sit by your left leg (have you been to Obedience school?). "Good dog." Step forward. The instant there's a pull, stop and go through the routine again. Your daily walks may take forever and get nowhere for a few days, but he'll get it eventually. Another way to cure pulling is to use a head collar such as the Halti or Promise, or the No-Pull harness-type device.

Prevention: A dog pulls by leaning into the collar only as hard as it takes to propel the dog and owner forward. Begin as you mean to continue and do not let a puppy pull.

Question: "Our ten-week-old Golden Retriever is fine during the day, but gets into everything at night—stealing clothes, towels, eyeglasses, etc. She has plenty of toys to occupy her. I'm about ready to stick her outside at night. Do you think Obedience classes would help?"

Answer: This very young puppy doesn't need toys or other entertainment at night! She needs the security and comfort of a *crate!* (see Chapter 1). Get into puppy kindergarten classes as fast as you can.

Prevention: Crate train and confine!

Question: "Our Sheltie is two years old and still jumps up on people. He did well in training classes, but we have to hold him in a Sit/Stay when greeting guests."

Answer: The dog did well in training so perhaps he does not fully understand about being on a Sit/Stay when greeting anyone. And that's the clue: *anyone,* not just guests.

Prevention: Give this dog attention only when he's sitting nicely. That rule goes for everyone. Each family member must take the time to make the dog do a Sit/Stay before saying hello, before and during petting, before feeding and before playing. Jumping up earns Ignoring. Second offense, a Time-out.

Question: "We can't keep our German Shepherd off the furniture. Sometimes he slinks off the couch as we walk into the room and he looks really guilty, but he's right back up as soon as our backs are turned. What can we do?"

Answer: One solution is to keep dog and couch in separate rooms! Your mistake was to let the unsupervised dog have access to forbidden furniture the first time. That's not guilt. The dog connects the couch with punishment, and since he doesn't get killed for doing it, he returns to his creature comfort ASAP. There are several devices on the market (ScatMat is one) to make a correction when you are home but can't watch the dog. When you go out, confine the dog to a couchless, furnitureless room.

Prevention: If dogs on furniture are not your style, then the darling puppy should not be allowed on any furniture at all, *ever,* not even once.

Question: "I own a Toy Fox Terrier and a large tabby cat. How can I train the dog not to eat the cat feces in the litter box? It's an indoor cat that must use the box."

Answer: My own theory (totally unscientific) on this fairly common cat/dog problem is that the odor of fish in cat excrement makes it more appealing to dogs. Your best bet is to get a litter box with a cover and place the opening in such a way that the cat has access, but not the dog.

Prevention: Start off with the litter box in a spot the dog can't reach, perhaps in the basement or anywhere only the cat can get to via a cat door.

Question: "When can a puppy be left home alone outside the confines of her crate? Is it advisable even then?"

Answer: Any crate-trained dog can be crated for up to four hours during the day when necessary. For a puppy, the next step is the run of a kitchen or other small room or area that can be closed off and cleared of anything that you would not leave a toddler alone with—electric cords, cleaning supplies, anything that could be pulled down (tablecloths and plants) or knocked over (trash and garbage). Leave the crate door hooked open or remove the door. When all is set, casually go in and out of the room every few minutes until the pup pays no attention to your arrival or departure. For some dogs (large ones that are destructive chewers, for example), confinement when left alone may be a way of life forever.

Prevention: No dog should go from crate confinement directly to the run of the house. When the pup is relaxed about being left alone in extended confinement (one room), that's progress. But if you take away this safety net too soon, the old problem of separation anxiety will land you both back at square one.

14

THOSE GOLDEN OLDIES

Old dogs represent many of our emotions rolled into one warm, four-legged, furry bundle. The good happy times shared, as well as the bad times and, always, the passage of time. The dog we grew up with has a very special place, and so does the dog with which *we* grow old. White muzzles and eyebrows bring warm smiles of acknowledgment from even the unknown passerby.

Owners of older dogs may face a different set of problems. Diminished sight, hearing, hair and mobility, failing health, changes in appetite, reactions to a change in the weather—and with all these things come certain changes in behavior, too. Sound familiar? Yes, all the same things we ourselves face in later years to a varying degree. But just because they are "normal" does not make them any less upsetting to the dog's owner.

Grow old along with me!
The best is yet to be.

—Robert Browning

SIGNS OF AGING—SEEN AND UNSEEN

There are also dogs who show almost no outward signs of the aging process, but need our care and protection as much as those that do. Their desire to please their owners with a display of vitality could be their undoing. Dogs don't complain, but a watchful owner spots the slight limp, the pawing at a troublesome tooth and the "ouch" in the spine going up or down stairs. A considerate owner knows when to slow down the walk, shorten the playtime, cut down on the physical exercise and eliminate the acrobatic tricks.

Some questions regarding elderly dogs that frequently come up are answered in the following pages. For an excellent scientific, but very readable, book on the subject, see *Senior Years—Understanding Your Dog's Aging Process* (Howell Book House, 1992) by John K. Hampton, Jr., Ph.D., and Suzanne H. Hampton, Ph.D.

Question: "My dog is now eleven years old and I, too, am a senior citizen. My problem concerns the expense of good veterinary care. I don't begrudge my vet the increases in the past few years, but it is tough on my minimal retirement income. Is there anything like Medicare for pets?"

Answer: There is pet health insurance. If your pet is healthy and has had normal veterinary care, you could look into it. The rates are based on the younger dog (from three months through nine years of age) with rates for older dogs averaging about fifty percent more, and there are the usual insurance deductibles and limits per injury or illness. On the other hand, most veterinarians either give across-the-board discounts to senior citizens or will adjust fees on an individual basis. They want to help you keep your pet healthy.

Prevention: Do look into pet health insurance when you first get your dog. Coverage in the United States does not include routine visits for immunizations or other preventive procedures, but does cover spaying or neutering. Whether you're a senior citizen or not, if you're having trouble meeting the fees, speak privately to your veterinarian, not the employee who writes up the bill. (Reducing scheduled fees requires an executive decision.)

Question: "Our mixed-breed dog has always run free, but on three occasions recently she has been brought home by neighbors who say she was acting strangely. They thought she might have been hit by a car, but we couldn't find any sign of it. She is fourteen years old and has always found her way home. What do you suppose is going on?"

Answer: If you want to give a label, try *senility*. It is not unusual for older dogs to become disoriented and "act strangely," often standing in the middle of the road, completely confused as to where they are or where they are going. Fourteen is definitely a senior citizen and no dogs, particularly older ones, should go out by themselves. Keep yours at home now in a fenced area or walk her on a leash.

Prevention: Oldtimers and immature youths are alike in many ways. Both need more care, more protection—leashes, fences and a watchful eye.

Question: "Our Collie, Willhe (for 'will he or won't he'), is almost twelve years old and has taken to growling if we touch him when he's sleeping. He never used to mind our petting him in his sleep. Do dogs go into a deeper sleep as they get older?"

Quiet times are good, too.

Answer: I don't know how deep a sleep older dogs enjoy, but many begin to snore loudly, which would indicate a good sound sleep. The culprit in your case, however, is more likely a loss of hearing, and the dog is startled by your silent touch. Let him sleep, or stamp your foot on the floor or clap your hands and be sure he's awake before stroking him. (Love that name!)

Prevention: Be sure a dog is awake before petting—a sensible rule no matter what the dog's age or hearing. It's an important safety rule to teach children—not to touch a dog that's asleep.

Question: "I have a Lhasa Apso. She is thirteen years old and has always been fed twice a day. Suddenly she has stopped eating her breakfast. The veterinarians say she's healthy and it's okay for her to eat one meal a day. I tried several different brands of food but she has no appetite."

Answer: Follow the doctors' orders! They know what's best for your dog. Part of the problem here is the guilt you are feeling at possibly not being a good provider. If it makes you feel better, and the dog goes along with the plan, feed her half her regular meal twice a day. Just don't start adding a little of this and a bit of that or you'll defeat the purpose!

Prevention: The geriatric dog's appetite slows down along with everything else in its system. Some do better on two half-portions, but old dogs often become obese because their owners can't resist adding little goodies. An appreciated substitute for mealtime is "massage grooming"—slow, steady brushing combined with a gentle massage. (Good, quiet therapy for dog owners, too.)

Question: "I've noticed a change in my dog's coat this winter. After the usual shedding, the coat never grew in as thick as usual. Could this be why he doesn't want to stay outdoors for more than a few minutes? He's twelve years old. We live in snow country."

Answer: Hair loss is common in older dogs and most noticeable in heavily coated breeds. This, combined with a normal decrease in the dog's ability to regulate its body temperature, is reason enough for the dog to be uncomfortable when outside in cold weather.

Prevention: There's nothing you can do to stop Father Time. Provide a manmade coat in the winter and dry the dog thoroughly when wet (rain or snow). Keep him out of the sun during the heat of the day in summer. Dogs of any age should be kept away from sources of both heat and cooling indoors.

Question: "When our Golden Retriever was about seven, we cut back on his daily walks and general exercise. He's nine and now we are told he is obese and needs more exercise! How much exercise is enough; how much is too much?"

Answer: It's a question that can only be answered on an individual basis. It's not a one-size-fits-all situation. The fact that your dog is overweight indicates both problems: He's overfed and underexercised. But how much is "over" and how much "under"? That's the individual riddle. Go with your vet's recommendation regarding food, and increase your daily walks gradually. You should see a difference on the scale in about three months.

Prevention: Maintaining an optimum weight in a dog is not nearly so hard as doing it yourself! After all, the dog doesn't raid the fridge, stop for ice cream after the movies or prepare snacks for TV time. No, the dog waits for *you* to dole out the main course and all the extras.

Question: "I have two dogs, one is four and the other seven years old. They are very well behaved although they've never had formal Obedience training. I'd like to get involved in Obedience now, but I've been told they are too old. True?"

Answer: Not a bit! Older dogs usually enjoy the social aspect of classes as much as the added attention they get from the training. Keep it fun. And if there are some things your dogs just don't get, no one will mind if you do it their way. One of my own geriatric ex-show dogs does the entire heeling exercise very nicely except that she will not sit on lead, so we do it her way. When all the other dogs sit, she's given the command "stand." Good dog!

Prevention: All mature dogs (well behaved or not, formally trained or not) have long since picked up all they need to know to get along, so it may take them longer to catch on to learning by rote. Some things have to be *un*learned first. For example, you may have taught your dogs *Down* to mean "don't jump up." In training parlance that word is *Off,* and *Down* means "belly up to the floor." Patience.

Question: "We're going to Europe this summer for three weeks, leaving our dog in a boarding kennel. She's a sweet old thing, but has not been well for the past year. Would it be uncaring to tell the owner of the kennel and my vet not to use any heroic measures to save her if she becomes seriously ill?"

Answer: It would be appropriate, caring and kind.

Prevention: We can't put our lives on hold, but we can plan ahead for our pets by accepting responsibility for all realistic possibilities. This is a case in point.

Question: "My sister has to be in a rehabilitation center for about three months, during which time I'll be caring for her five-year-old Sheltie. She lives for that dog. Would it be okay to ask if I could let her see her dog once or twice while she's there? I know it's not possible in hospitals because we've just gone through six weeks of that."

Answer: Not only okay, but you may find yourself visiting many additional patients every time you go! Nursing homes, rehabilitation centers and—at the other end of the scale, children's facilities—all have witnessed the miraculous improvement in patients when they are allowed to touch, hold or just look at a dog.

Prevention: None. So long as the dog is friendly, outgoing, obedient and healthy (no fleas, please), go for it!

Question: "I have spent over a year looking for an apartment that will let me keep Misty, my ten-year-old Keeshond. The few landlords who will accept pets allow only small dogs (under twenty pounds). What is a senior citizen supposed to do when his only family is his dog?"

Answer: If there is no way to keep the dog, contact the specific breed rescue group (information is available locally from a breeder or from the American Kennel Club). They understand the problem and are there to help. In the case of an infirm or sickly older dog, or a dog that would be under extreme stress in a new home, the kindest thing to consider is euthanasia. Not an easy decision, but caring.

Prevention: Not everyone who must live in an apartment wants a cat or a bowl of fish. It's a nationwide dilemma and seems particularly harsh when all human/animal studies prove the mental, physical and emotional benefits senior citizens derive from dog ownership.

It's time to educate landlords about dogs. A lease clause would make a tenant fully responsible for the behavior of the dog; an area could be set aside for dogs to be walked on leash, and provided with plastic bags and receptacles for cleanup, as is done in many parks now. Rules regarding dogs in elevators, on lobby furniture or whatever applies would not be out of line.

Question: "What interesting things can an older dog do? Most activities like ball chasing, jogging, hiking and keeping up with the kids are geared to the puppy and young dog. My dog is thirteen and still bright and perky but has a touch of arthritis, and the vet suggested we slow down her active life."

Answer: Look into doing therapy work. If she's good with kids, there are lots of children's hospitals in need of the therapeutic benefits from visiting dogs, as well as rehabilitation centers, nursing homes and veterans' hospitals. Start on this and you won't have a spare minute to wonder what your dog can do.

Sit in the sun and watch your local school's practice sessions (soccer, football, field hockey, etc.). In warm weather, make it a slow stroll along the beach, lake, stream or other previous romping ground. Any dog that was an expert hunter in younger years could retire to snooze on the bank and become an expert fisherman!

Prevention: There's no way to prevent arthritis, of course, although there are drugs to help ease the pain. But there are plenty of ways to stop the mind from stagnating.

A walk and a snooze. Perfect!

WHO, WHAT AND WHERE

AMERICAN KENNEL CLUB, INC.
51 Madison Avenue
New York, NY 10010
Tel: (212) 696-8200

A.S.P.C.A.
424 East 92nd Street
New York, NY 10128
Tel: (212) 876-7700

THE DELTA SOCIETY
(Resource for Human/Animal
Interactions)
321 Burnett Avenue South
Renton, WA 98055
Tel: (206) 226-7357

MEDIPET
P.O. Box 94314
Seattle, WA 98124-9781
Tel: (800) 528-4961

MORRIS ANIMAL FOUNDATION
45 Inverness Drive East
Englewood, CO 80112
Tel: (303) 790-2345

NATIONAL ANIMAL INTEREST
ALLIANCE
P.O. Box 66579
Portland, OR 97290

NATIONAL ASSN of DOG OBEDIENCE
INSTRUCTORS (NADOI)
2286 East Steel Road
St. Johns, MI 48879
(Send S.A.S.E. for information)

NATIONAL DOG REGISTRY
(Tattoo Registry)
P.O. Box 116
Woodstock, NY 12498
Tel: (914) 679-BELL

THERAPY DOGS
INTERNATIONAL
6 Hilltop Road
Mendham, NJ 07945
Tel: (201) 543-0888

UNITED KENNEL CLUB
100 East Kilgore Road
Kalamazoo, MI 49001
Tel: (616) 343-9020

K-9 COUNTERCONDITIONING
(audio tape for noise fears)
1321 Longmeadow Drive
Glenview, IL 60025
Tel: (800) 952-6517

PET-AGREE and TATTLE TALE
K-11 Enterprises
P.O. Box 306
Camillus, NY 13031
Tel: (800) OBEY-ME

GLOSSARY

AKC: The American Kennel Club.

adopted dog: One acquired from a private or government-run shelter; may be purebred or mixed breed. (See *rescued dog.*)

aggressive: Term describing a dog that attacks or bites without provocation. This is an overused term, often referring incorrectly to a bossy or assertive personality.

assertiveness: The attitude of a "bossy" dog, often a "teenager."

barking: Dog talk. It may be minimal, moderate or excessive—just like people talk.

benched show: A dog show where dogs are kept on raised benches when not being shown or exercised. Nice for spectators, but now almost extinct.

bite inhibition: What every dog must learn: how hard to bite down and on what. Pups begin to learn it at about four to six weeks.

biting: 100% unacceptable behavior.

bitter apple: Repellent to prevent unwanted licking or chewing.

bonding: The trust and understanding developed between dog and owner.

Book According to Dogs: A mythical canine codex; only dogs are certain of its contents.

breed rescue: Breed clubs active in placement of purebred dogs in need of a new home. A donation is expected, or a fee charged.

CD, CDX, UD, UDX, OTCH: AKC Obedience titles earned at AKC Trials after much dedicated work and training. (Companion Dog, Companion Dog Excellent, Utility Dog, Utility Dog Excellent and Obedience Trial Champion.)

CGC: Canine Good Citizen title given by the AKC, for passing a test that includes basic skills necessary for a good companion.

canine seat belts: A canine version of our own car safety belts.

caprophagy: The eating of excrement.

chew, *v.*: What all dogs do in order to eat, exercise their jaws or pass the time (or destroy the couch).

chew, *n.*: Any toy meant to be chewed (not the couch).

coat: The dog's natural hair. Or, a man–made article of canine clothing to keep the dog warm, dry—or just handsome.

confinement: Any restricted area where the dog is safe from danger or from punishment.
crate: The dog's very own place: a bed, safe den or home away from home.

dam: The female canine parent.
dog/bitch: In dog parlance, "dog" is the male, "bitch" is the female.
dog run: A securely fenced limited area (usually rectangular) in which a dog may safely exercise. May be roofed with fence material for the climber.
dominant dog: A dog in charge, whose roles of dog and owner are reversed.
Down: The most incorrectly used command; means "*Lie* down" but never "*Get* down." (See *Off.*)
dual champion: A dog with a championship in Conformation and one in Field Trials.

fear biting: A temperament flaw. The dog appears to be fearful, then suddenly attacks, apparently without provocation.
fear period: A phase that most dogs go through at about five months of age and sometimes again about five months later.
flight space: The distance from (usually strange) people, other dogs or objects that every dog needs so as not to feel threatened. A tight leash negates this space.

gait: The dog's pattern of footsteps at different speeds.

heeling: Walking with the dog alongside your left leg.
herding dogs: A group of breeds used to herd livestock.
hounds: Dogs used to hunt by sight *or* scent.
housetraining: Teaching the dog where to eliminate—and where *not* to.

ignoring: A discipline, or teaching tool.

kibble: Dry dog food.
KPT: Kindergarten Puppy Training. Obedience and socializing for pups up to five months of age. Great!

licking: An annoying habit; if severe (self-mutilating), requires prompt veterinary attention.

marking territory: Depositing drops of urine to let subsequently passing dogs know that "Rufus was here." Normal male activity.

mixed-breed: Any dog whose sire and dam are not of the same breed or any dog of unknown origin ("It looks like" is a mixed breed).

mouthing: Generally a puppy activity; a leftover from nursing. Undesirable beyond puppyhood.

neutering: Surgical removal of the male's reproductive organs.

Non-Sporting: An AKC designation that includes recognized breeds that are primarily companion dogs today. The other AKC Groups are Sporting, Hound, Working, Terrier, Toy and Herding.

Obedience classes: Essential basic canine education. Can lead to higher levels of distinction and Obedience titles.

"Off": Command meaning "*Get* off." Not to be confused with "Down."

"old" dog: Small dogs generally live longer than giant breeds, so age alone does not determine senior citizenship.

pack: Three or more dogs operating as a unit. (Two dogs make a brace.) Dogs include humans in their pack.

pads: Soles of a dog's feet.

pedigree: Written genealogical record of a dog, with at least three generations.

proof training: Testing a dog's response to Obedience commands under distracting circumstances.

puppy: Technically, refers to a dog under 12 months of age, but mentally and physically most dogs are not mature until the age of two or, in some breeds or individuals, three years. Sort of like kids.

rescue(d) dog: A dog obtained from a Breed Rescue Service; sometimes used to refer to a found or adopted dog.

saturation: A means of overcoming many unwanted behaviors by overexposure to the cause.

shots: Immunizations against common canine diseases. "Permanent shots" is a misnomer. They are "adult" shots and must be renewed yearly.

sire: The male canine parent.

soft mouth: The gentle hold of bird or game by Sporting dogs.

spaying: Surgical removal of the bitch's reproductive organs.

sporting dogs: Dogs that hunt, such as Setters, Spaniels and Retrievers.

submissive urination: A form of submissive body language, not intentional misconduct.

TDI: Therapy Dog International, a title given to dogs that pass specific requirements to visit hospitals, nursing homes, etc., as designated by the TDI organization.

Terriers: Dogs used originally to hunt and dispatch vermin. From the Latin *terra*.

time-out: A discipline, or teaching tool.

toys: 1—Refers to all the very small breeds.

2—Inanimate playthings.

training collar: Any type of collar used for specific training, but generally referring to the "choke" or "slip" collar, which is briefly tightened around the dog's neck by the trainer to make a correction and immediately loosened. Should not be worn except during training sessions.

walk, *v.***:** What you do when you take the dog outside to eliminate; also, what you and the dog do to get some exercise.

walk, *n.***:** An event the dog enjoys by using all his senses.

working dogs: Dogs that originally pulled carts, or did other work such as guarding, hauling, racing or rescue.

CHECK POINTS

Here are names, addresses and suggestions for digging deeper into a variety of unusual dog-related topics available to anyone interested in dogs.

AMERICAN KENNEL CLUB, INC.
51 Madison Avenue
New York, NY 10010
(General Information)
(212) 696-8200
(212) 696-8245
(The AKC Library is here.)

or, for print materials, registrations, etc.:

AMERICAN KENNEL CLUB, INC.
5580 Centerview Drive
Raleigh, NC 27606
(919) 233-9780

A.S.P.C.A.
424 East 92nd Street
New York, NY 10128
(212) 876-7700

THE DELTA SOCIETY
(Resource for Human/Animal Interactions)
321 Burnett Ave. South
Renton, WA 98055
(206) 226-7357

ALPHA AFFILIATES, INC.
103 Washington St., Suite 362
Morristown, NJ 07960-6813
(For a Durable Power of Attorney for Pet Care to keep with your Will, send $2.00 plus a self-addressed, stamped business-size envelope.)

MEDIPET (Pet Health Insurance)
P.O. Box 94314
Seattle, WA 98124-9781
(800) 528-4961

MORRIS ANIMAL FOUNDATION
45 Inverness Dr. East
Englewood, CO 80112
(303) 790-2345

NATIONAL ANIMAL INTEREST ALLIANCE
P.O. Box 66579
Portland, OR 97290

NATIONAL ASSOCIATION of DOG OBEDIENCE INSTRUCTORS (NADOI)
2286 East Steel Road
St. Johns, MI 48879
(Send S.A.S.E. for information.)

NATIONAL DOG REGISTRY
(Tattoo Registry)
P.O. Box 116
Woodstock, NY 12498
(800) NDR-DOGS

THERAPY DOGS INTERNA-
TIONAL
1317 Fourth Avenue
Schenectady, NY 12303
(518) 429-0670

UNITED KENNEL CLUB
100 East Kilgore Road
Kalamazoo, MI 49001
(616) 343-9020

NATIONAL ASSOCIATION OF
PROFESSIONAL PET SITTERS
1200 G Street, NW, Suite 760
Washington, DC 20005
(800) 296-PETS
(For a list of pet sitters in your
area who are all bonded, insured
and have signed a Code of
Ethics.)

AMERICAN VETERINARY
MEDICAL ASSOCIATION
930 North Meacham Road
Schaumburg, IL 60196-1074
(The place to write for a list of
accredited schools if you'd like
to become a vet.)

UNITED STATES DOG AGILITY
ASSOCIATION
P.O. Box 850955
Richardson, TX 75085-0955
(214) 231-9700

DOGS FOR THE DEAF
(800) 990-DOGS
(One of numerous organizations
throughout the United States
and Canada that train dogs for
the hard-of-hearing.)

GUIDING EYES FOR THE BLIND
611 Granite Springs Road
Yorktown Heights, NY 10598
(914) 245-4024

SEEING EYE GUIDE DOGS FOR
THE BLIND
P.O. Box 375
Morristown, NJ 07963
(201) 539-4425

DOG WRITERS' ASSOCIATION
OF AMERICA
Salley Cooper, Secretary
222 Woodchuck Lane
Harwinton, CT 06791
(For membership and general
information, an annual writing
contest and the Dog Writers'
Educational Trust, which offers
scholarships to young people
involved with dogs.)

Videos

The AKC now has videotapes on
every conceivable subject involving dogs, including some for
children. Write or call for a list.
(919) 233-9780
(919) 233-9767

To order:

IN-SIGHT COMMUNICATIONS
19 Ketchum Street
Westport, CT 06880
The Westminster Kennel Club's 100th Anniversary Show—$45.00.

DORAL PUBLISHING, INC.
8650 SW Salish Lane, Suite 300
Wilsonville, OR 97070-9612
(503) 682-3307
Many titles on breeding and showing purebred dogs.

Audio Cassettes

K-9 COUNTERCONDITIONING
1321 Longmeadow Drive
Glenview, IL 60025
(800) 952-6517
Audio cassette to overcome noise fears.

THE CANINE CONSULTANT
P.O. Box 5044
Westport, CT 06881
(203) 454-4300

One-hour cassettes: Welcome Home, Puppy; Puppy Grows Up; Your Dog's Final Years; more.

PET-AGREE and TATTLE TALE
K-11 Enterprises
P.O. Box 306
Camillus, NY 13031
1 (800) OBEY-ME
Behavior modification and training devices, based on the dog's response to sound.

FOR FURTHER READING

Dog Owner's Home Veterinary Handbook, Delbert G. Carlson, DVM & James M. Giffin, MD (Howell Book House, 1993).

Dogs & Kids: Parenting Tips, Bardi McLennan (Howell Book House, 1993).

The Hijacking of the Humane Movement, Rod and Patti Strand (Doral Publishing, 1993).

Complete Dog Book (AKC) (Howell Book House, 1992).

INDEX